Cosmic Connections

Ancient Knowledge Meets Spiritual Science

DR. CHERI ST. ARNAULD

BALBOA
PRESS

A DIVISION OF HAY HOUSE

Balboa Press books may be ordered through booksellers or by contacting:

Balboa Press
A Division of Hay House
1663 Liberty Drive
Bloomington, IN 47403
www.balboapress.com
1 (877) 407-4847

Because of the dynamic nature of the Internet, any web addresses or
links contained in this book may have changed since publication and
may no longer be valid. The views expressed in this work are solely those
of the author and do not necessarily reflect the views of the publisher,
and the publisher hereby disclaims any responsibility for them.

The author of this book does not dispense medical advice or prescribe the use
of any technique as a form of treatment for physical, emotional, or medical
problems without the advice of a physician, either directly or indirectly. The
intent of the author is only to offer information of a general nature to help you
in your quest for emotional and spiritual well-being. In the event you use any
of the information in this book for yourself, which is your constitutional right,
the author and the publisher assume no responsibility for your actions.

Any people depicted in stock imagery provided by Thinkstock are models,
and such images are being used for illustrative purposes only.
Certain stock imagery © Thinkstock.

Printed in the United States of America.

ISBN: 978-1-4525-9067-7 (sc)
ISBN: 978-1-4525-9068-4 (hc)
ISBN: 978-1-4525-9066-0 (e)

Library of Congress Control Number: 2014900728

Balboa Press rev. date: 02/03/2014

To Archangel Raziel, who says this knowingness, this information, is no longer a mystery. The time has come for all to have a basic understanding of the universe and our spiritual connection to live with intent for the greatest good of all.

Contents

Acknowledgments

Many people were instrumental in this journey into cosmic connections. First, I thank Dr. Doris Christopher for being my soul sister, book editor, and friend. I also thank James Tyberonn for knowing without a doubt that there was a book in me. I also want to thank my children, Eva and Cole, whom I credit for my strength and wisdom in the world.

Introduction

Through an incredible journey of discovery, you will uncover connections between spirituality, science, and the ancient sacred teachings of old. Your journey will be one of personal insight as you contemplate food for thought, frame your own definition of spirituality, and consider connections that may apply to your life today and in the future. These pages will lay out a path that asks for your inner discernment to consider your worldview, new possibilities, and the best road toward living a centered life. You will embark on a trek through time, reviewing the lost teachings of Atlantis and the law of One, string theory, cocreation, sacred geometry, environmental disruptors that affect energy fields, meditation, the pineal gland, and energy healing to weave a web of spiritual understanding that builds a deeper reflection of your connected existence to Source, to each other, and to mother earth. This path asks you to consider not only your own individual walk but to reach out to help humanity as a whole as a way to bring purpose and meaning to your life.

The definition of "spirituality," as it is used here is not built on traditional religious teachings. It is built on a personal connection to universal Source through the lens of ancient teachings and scientific breakthroughs regarding new ways to view the universe and our role in the beautiful dance of life. Spirituality cultivates a relationship that holds us to the interconnected web of all things, revering the role of service to others as well as a focus on self, and viewing that service from a truly shared consciousness. This service flows from a realization that all are completely interconnected into one universal Source, and understanding every move we make, thought we have, and emotion we express will bring the same back to us. Service can be filled with compassion and appreciation for all living things on the earth.

These pages guide you on a journey to discover the relationship between spirituality, understanding connections between the soul and nature, and living within the universal flow of energy. Your journey through this book is but an introduction to a path of understanding to cocreate your own best world and consider a simple way of life that can change your thoughts and, allow you to develop a shared vision to attain this world for all humanity ... and ultimately for yourselves.

May your days be filled with receiving that which you give!

Namaste.

CHAPTER 1

A Look at Spirituality

I know that I am intelligent because
I know that I know nothing.
—Socrates

This book is designed to be a primer or, if you will, an introduction to a variety of concepts people on alternative spiritual paths have discovered, discussed, and studied for years. One could truly argue that Eastern religions, native cultures, and others have known and worked with many of these concepts from the time the ancients came upon the earth. But we get ahead of ourselves. Practitioners and scientists have brought most of this conventional wisdom back to the surface in the past century as science comes ever closer to intertwining spiritual concepts. The momentum for people to seek additional understanding of spiritual and scientific knowledge is beginning to gain momentum again. Scientific research is garnering support for meditation, a collective consciousness, and a changing reality based on the way one perceives reality. Studies in physics, quantum mechanics, microbiology, genetics, and mathematics prove how much we still do not know about the makeup of the universe. Our bodies, minds, thoughts, DNA, and emotions—in fact, all mysteries on earth and in space—are stunning in their interconnectedness. What we are learning completely boggles the mind.

As we each consider what spirituality looks like in our personal lives, let us consider that spirituality should be embedded within our personal worldview, the way we approach life and deal with others every day. Spirituality is defined here as a personal relationship, a connection of the heart, a coherent expression of love from you to the universal Source of all that is. This one-on-one relationship is very different and very personal for each of us, but it is the same in its personal connection to Source. This simple definition, how to connect to Source and what Source is, holds several assumptions for many people. It is not necessary everyone think or believe the same way. In fact, it has never been more important than it is today to develop your beliefs based on your insights and intuitions.

This discovery of connections to science and ancient teachings is simply one way to holistically build a broader understanding of our human selves in relation to what we have learned from science and the universe as a whole and our place in the divine pattern. Spirituality should not simply be a window dressing or a feel-good attempt to label oneself without considering how to be a better person. It should be something that can take priority with intention each day to live life through a continuous vibration of love that draws strength in its coherent connection from the heart to Source. Living within this vibration of love, which is an actual measurable energy field around all things, will be explored in future chapters. But for now, it is also the energy that when focused can drive us to live a life of love that could impact our view of the world and our desire to build a community embracing all people.

Spirituality is not simply going to church, temple, or synagogue, or meditating or praying. Spirituality may also be a way of viewing the world as everyone completely interconnected with each other through waves of energy that unite us as one. It is true that spirituality and religion should be united, as all religions would consider spiritual teachings and hope to provide guidance to their parishioners. But in the same breath, we also know there are very religious people in the world, learned in doctrine, who are not necessarily spiritual in their presentation and connections with others. And there are people who consider themselves to be very spiritual, who exhibit their inner spirituality as an outward expression in their approach to life, but they do not follow any specific religious doctrine. Spirituality should be something we practice both inwardly in our connection between our heart and Source and outwardly through daily living. Most important, it should be something exhibited to everyone we come in contact with each day. It is not meant for a select few.

Having a personal sense of spiritual practice can truly be the link to finding purpose in our lives. Yet people are busy in their daily activities, and many would say they do not have time to be spiritual or develop a practice to build and strengthen their connection to Source. They work too hard, have too many responsibilities, or simply cannot think about one more thing. How can we take the time to embed something else within our daily routines? As we continue our journey to understand our soul's connection to nature, we may ask how we cannot take the time to embed something new into our routines. The difference it could make in our lives, as we will see, is startling.

This renewed desire to understand a different, personal, spiritual path and seek a new spiritual truth is not necessarily based in one traditional religion. *Cosmic Connections* is not a history lesson in Christianity, but some brief history is important. The Old Testament existed for thousands of years prior to the birth of Christ, yet Western religions generally see it as preparation for the new covenant, or New Testament. However, various forms of Christianity were practiced for over three hundred years after the crucifixion. All followed some early recorded memory of the teachings of Jesus, often seen through the eyes of one of the twelve disciples. "Christianity in the ancient world was much more diverse than it is now, with a number of gospels circulating in addition to the four that were finally collected into the New Testament," noted Bart Ehrman, chairman of religious studies at the University of North Carolina. "Eventually, one point of view prevailed and the others were declared heresy," he said, "including the Gnostics who believed that salvation depended on secret knowledge that Jesus imparted."

The Roman emperor Constantine the Great influenced the first unified Christian church 325 years after the crucifixion, when he took action and brought together 318 bishops from across the Roman Empire to find common ground for the church. He brought them to the Turkish city of Nicea and ultimately developed what Christianity is today by creating and signing the statement of compromise known as the Nicene Creed. This formed the basis for Christian ideology. Whether they selected the four gospels in the New Testament or not is still debated, but the newly found lost gospels of Thomas, Judas, and even Mary of Magdala are more closely tied to Gnostic beliefs in early Christianity than the four gospels currently in the New Testament.

The Greek word *gnosis* means, in essence, "secret knowledge," or knowledge of transcendence arrived at through internal, intuitive means. But gnosis was also thought to mean "emancipation" or a "oneness with God." Gnosticism relies on personal religious experience as its primary authority. Early Christian Gnostics did adopt their own versions of authoritative scriptures, such as those found in the Library of Nag Hammadi, a town in upper Egypt, near ancient Chenoboskion, where thirteen codices were discovered around 1945. The Nag Hammadi Codex XIII is a papyrus codex with a collection of early Christian Gnostic texts in an ancient Sahidic dialect. Gnosticism has an extensive and much debated history throughout the world, and the definitions and interpretations of Gnosticism are far too much information to place in an introductory chapter of this book. However, in 1979, Elaine Pagels, professor of religion at Princeton University, published *The Gnostic Gospels*, which detailed how early bishops of the Christian church suppressed some of the writings found at Nag Hammadi.

An important Gnostic text found in 1773 is also significant to mention here. It is called the Pistis Sophia and believed written between the third and fourth centuries CE. The text proclaims Jesus remained on earth for eleven years after the resurrection and taught his disciples up to the first level of the "mystery," or the descent and ascent of the soul. Sophia is the female divinity of Gnosticism and the divine feminine, or the female aspect, of the Holy Spirit. The Pistis Sophia is known as the book of the Savior and is an early text of Christian writings. The Pistis Sophia is a blend of primitive Christianity and Hellenic paganism with elements of reincarnation, astrology, mystery, and Hermetic magic. It includes women in the dialogue in ways that later Christianity would never allow.

About the same time the Gnostic gospels were discovered, the Dead Sea Scrolls were found in the Qumran caves along the Dead Sea. The Dead Sea Scrolls are thought to have been written by the Essenes, an ancient Jewish sect that lived a sacred, spiritual, almost monk-like existence. The Essenes were both male and female and believed to have existed from about the third century BCE to about the third century CE. The scrolls were said to hold the oldest Hebrew text of the Bible. The content of the scrolls are not widely publicized and are currently held mostly within the research community. The majority of the texts are actually not biblical in nature but thought to be a collection of the Essenes' beliefs. Science authenticated the dating and authenticity of these documents.

Traditional religion has always invoked a belief based on faith alone. Science is finally bringing forth some interesting data and information that may allow us to view things slightly differently yet again. *Cosmic Connections* does not refute the Bible or any underlying belief of any one religion or movement. To reiterate, the purpose here is not to tie spirituality to any one religion or religious movement but to define spirituality as simply a very personal one-on-one connection between the heart and God. In fact, most religions have the same basic premise. But perhaps asking individuals to depend on faith alone has left many to fiercely fight about whose set of practices and beliefs are right and whose are wrong. Perhaps the time has come, and we have evolved spiritually enough, to begin to look at the blend of what we know and what we believe. It may not be the leaders of the churches who will embrace the scientific evidence that may change some of the interpretations or long-held beliefs of sacred writings. It could be the people who have opened their hearts and minds to blend scientific information and sacred writings into a new spiritual way of life. It may be the people who are ready to forgo who is right and who is wrong and simply say let us practice being who we need to be in the world based on love. Is that not the core of all religions? Love all thy neighbors as thyself? This one saying may have been the most fundamental and most important thing we should have been doing all these years. And now, science is telling us why!

Many of the ideas discussed in this book could be perceived as coming straight out of new age or new thought texts. It is true many ancient ideas were founded in sacred writings of Eastern religions or knowledge channeled from entities known to communicate with masters and archangels in the world of ether. Yet in the next breath, we also acknowledge current physicists discussing parallel dimensions existing along with our own and quantum physicists talking about how reality does not exist at all, that reality only exists in our mind's eye. Science now sounds as "out there" as the mystics of today or of old. This book is a blend of mystical sacred concepts and teachings, whether received through ancient Vedic writings or channeled from masters in another realm. Combined with startling scientific knowledge around quantum physics, reality, and healing practices, it leaves us with a thread of truth for spirituality to reign, all working for the highest good of humanity.

Using the mystical blended with the scientific can provide a new way to view our old core programming and subconscious mind that holds us each separate and apart from one another, saying, "Take care of number one." The time has possibly come for us to view the world through love that is less centered on ourselves. It is time to look to a conscious Oneness with universal Source through compassion, kindness, giving, and doing no harm as a better way of life on earth. Spirituality may require more than just spiritual knowledge, as this does not always equate to *being* spiritual. It is perhaps a way of life that every day leads us to connect our heart with Source. In the following pages, we see how the energy and effort we expend in the world will bring the same energy back to us.

So another sense of being spiritual could also be serving others and doing no harm to others as ways to serve ourselves. Many people believe they live in love or are helping others. But if the relationship hurts another in an unintended way, it could be an ego-driven love that does not come from the heart.

Most important, connecting with our environment and community will help us gain our greatest growth as we learn to give first and trust that the rest will come. The timing may be right for us to consider a new understanding of the energies of the universe and our spiritual connection therein to live with daily purpose for the greatest good for all humanity. Spirituality may be a way of being one with nature and preserving all the earth offers to us. Perhaps in totality, spirituality is what we *are* that counts.

True spirituality may be tied to our current understanding of universal law, sacred geometry, the laws of physics, and living within a shared consciousness. It is part of the life force embedded in all. Most important, maybe spirituality means considering the Golden Rule as the most important teaching in the world. This is the common spiritual saying for all people, regardless of faith. It is written in some form in at least thirteen religions, "Do unto others as you would have done to you." The Golden Rule is defined as the ethic of reciprocity that conceptually describes the relationship between self and others in an equal ethical fashion. This rule is often thought of as the most concise and general principle or rule of ethical conduct and may be the true foundation of shared spirituality.

Each of the chapters in this book could be an individual book in themselves. Indeed, entire college curriculums could be built on each and every concept, with internships and dedicated practice included to fully understand and utilize the information. Even the sources used in the book are a blend of scientific research and current alternative thinkers. The hope is that this brief overview may spark some interest and inner knowing for people to continue on their own path of discovery and enlightenment and to delve deeper into the areas that intrigued them the most. The goal here is to build connections between science and beliefs that may hold a very personal truth for each of us. Then we can weave a thread of reason to encourage this time of now to begin practicing a way of being in the world that will create the best life for all humanity and, thereby, our best lives! It is time for us to take back our power, to trust our own counsel and intuition, and to follow our own paths. Most important, as we enter a new spiritual age, it is time to live our own truth. If we want to create a new world for ourselves, we must consider our impact in the world and how we affect others. We are connected globally, indeed universally; there is no other way.

Food for Thought

Try keeping an open mind, and approach the content in this book through a lens of possibility. It is possible to hold an idea that challenges our world view without having to believe all aspects.

Think about developing your own statement of spirituality. One simple definition of spirituality has been identified in this chapter. Perhaps create a very simple statement of the meaning and purpose of spirituality in your life as a framework for reading the rest of this book.

CHAPTER 2

The Law of One

In the beginning was the Word, and the Word
was with God, and the Word was God.
—John 1:1

There is only one breath. All are made of the
same clay. The light within all is the same.
—Guru Granth Sahib

As we begin our journey and contemplate the thought that we are all interconnected within our hearts and souls, it is necessary to review the teachings of the law of One and how this concept may be important in spirituality. The law of One is an ancient, sacred science describing the conscious Oneness of all things within the infinite intelligent universe. All Oneness, all consciousness is intelligent energy and stems from the God Source, Great Spirit, Universal Spirit, whatever you call the supreme intelligence of which we all belong. This oneness is a vibration, a frequency that reigns throughout the universe, and this frequency is love. There is a difference between the emotions of love as we understand it and the frequency of love that is the vibration of the conscious Oneness of all things. Some say the law of One was first experienced as the unalterable universal truth and way of life of several ancient civilizations, including the Lemurian and early Atlantean people, who are believed to be two of the oldest civilizations on earth. The way of life or eternal intention of the law of One was expressed as love, respect for free will, and perpetual life creation. The law of One means being in harmony with, one with, and a servant of Universal Consciousness.

In fact, in pure form, the law of One is all that is. There is no right or wrong; there is only beingness or one continuous flow of frequency consciousness. Within this flow of consciousness, we each are a spark of the whole, with free will to build a life and express that life as we choose. Our free will, our individual expression of this frequency, allows us to create the reality we experience on this planet. Our individual expression, our creation of our own life is, of course, based on other universal facts as well, such as scientific and mathematical laws. But for now, consider that the entire creation or universe is simply made of two things: pattern or mathematics, and consciousness. Mathematicians are discovering amazing things that defy traditional thinking as we know it, allowing us to view the fractal world in startling, new ways. Science also supports our ability to cocreate our own lives and, in essence, our own reality through the quantum field. Each of these will be explored as we discover how closely we are all tied together as one.

As a spiritual spark of the One, living on the earth, we are free to express our life, our love frequency, the creator's essence as we choose. It is hard to fully comprehend that some would choose to express an intelligent love essence through negative emotions and actions. If we look around us, we see people making this choice every day. Yet in the law of One, all choices are allowed. We can choose to remain on a path toward becoming highly spiritual beings resonating at a high level of love consciousness. Or we can express our free will in negative, hurtful, and destructive ways. The primary key to living in this vibration is practicing the frequency of love from a place without ego. The "rule" of loving others before ourselves has been handed down through time. Do unto others as you would have done to you. The choice is and always has been ours.

The law of One also says all things in the universe exist intrinsically, because in the beginning, there was one omnipotent frequency or original thought, which was known as the word. Everything that exists everywhere—every planet, every star, all things on planet earth, the wind and sun, every emotion, every feeling, every aspect—are related through this one unified thought and its manifestation called creation. The law of One is quite simple. The universe is one original thought of the creator, and that thought was a vibration, the vibration of love. This one thought created all things in the universe, and all are connected together within this frequency of consciousness, because all things belong to the One. We are individual sparks in human bodies, living life on earth. Not everyone may agree with this. That is okay, because everyone is entitled to his or her point of view.

Native Americans have always known this, as they hold all nature, including water and air, are sacred. Legends say trees and people come from the same DNA, from earth. People need what the tree gives as it breathes, and the tree needs what we give as we breathe. When we treat all things as spirit, we begin to realize we are all one family. The world never ends; it only cycles.

> All things are connected. Whatever befalls the
> earth befalls the sons of the earth. Man did not
> weave the web of Life; he is only a strand in it.
> Whatever he does to the web, he does to himself.
> —Chief Seattle, Nez Perce, 1854

The premise is that what we do to others we also do to ourselves. All life on earth and outside the earthly realm is bound together in this conscious Oneness. The saying goes that when one is harmed, all are harmed, and when one is healed, all are healed. It is this basic belief that drives the law of reciprocity and the law of attraction in our lives. All is vibratory in nature, and all nature is tied within the vibration.

The Native American Whirling Rainbow prophecy has long held for Navajo and Hopi tribes the promise of peace for all nations and people. The Rainbow Foundation says, "The Rainbow Race stresses equality and opposes the idea of a superior race that would control or conquer other races. The Rainbow Race brings peace through the understanding that all races are one. The unity of all colors, all creeds working together for the good of the whole, is the idea that is embodied in the Whirling Rainbow. When all pathways to wholeness are respected by all cultures, the prophecy of the Whirling Rainbow will be complete." Images of the Whirling Rainbow are created in sand paintings—an ancient, sacred, healing picture—as the Whirling Rainbow Woman comes from all four directions and curves like a swastika, covering north, east, south, and west. It should be noted the swastika, while having terrible memories and connotations for people worldwide today, was actually an old and powerful symbol for many ancient religions and sacred writings. The symbol of the four-sided swastika is an archetype for the rotations of time and consciousness, moving clockwise and counterclockwise in upward or downward spirals, allowing souls to experience many levels of reality simultaneously. The word "swastika" comes from the Sanskrit words *su,* meaning well, and *asti,* meaning to be. It is hard for us to imagine that this symbol, representing so much death and horror at the hands of the Nazis in World War II, would actually be a symbol to revere without this horrible past.

According to the Whirling Rainbow Foundation, the Whirling Rainbow prophecy provides a vision for future generations.

> The prophecy of the Whirling Rainbow was very specific and said that when the time of the White Buffalo approaches, the third generation of the White Eyes' children will grow their hair and speak of love as the healer of the children of the earth. These children will seek new ways of understanding themselves and others. They will wear feathers and beads and paint their faces. They will seek the elders of the Red Race and drink of their wisdom. These white-eyed children will be a sign the ancestors are returning in white bodies, but they are red on the inside. They will learn to walk the Earth Mother in balance again and reform the ideas of the white chiefs. These children will be tested as they were when they were red ancestors, using unnatural substances like firewater to see if they can remain on the sacred path. Colorful dreams would be brought into the sleeptime and dreamtime dreams of these newborn warriors of the Rainbow, and they would begin to learn how to walk in balance. The changes in our Earth Mother would create fear in her children, which would later lead to the understanding and unity of our planet—one people.

The Whirling Rainbow prophecy reminds us a time will come, and hopefully soon, when all people will work together as one people, one human race here on earth.

A famous individual who made reference to the law of One quite extensively is the world-renowned Edgar Cayce. Edgar Cayce lived from 1877 to 1945 and was a channeler, seer, and healer, who channeled more than fourteen thousand psychic readings and over twenty-five hundred readings referring to the law of One in his extensive writings on Atlantis. While we do not have hard scientific evidence that Atlantis truly existed, Cayce was prolific about the Atlantean society and that period. He acknowledged the law of One as he channeled about the Golden Age of Atlantis, which reigned for thousands of years. Atlantis was originally led by a very spiritual society known as the law of One. Cayce described the earliest Atlanteans as being light forms, probably better understood as having a body of light, if you will. These light bodies vibrated at a very high frequency and maintained the highest levels of consciousness, ultimately connected to the one creator, God. They stayed true in belief that all are one.

Cayce talked at length about this ancient, very intelligent society and their technological progression over thousands of years that eventually led to their downfall. The people became fractured between the power of love and the love of power. They were masters at the use of crystal technology, which eventually led to massive explosions and the end of the Atlantean world. It is believed the people who survived the explosion took their knowledge to Egypt, South and North America, and Tibet. The ancient Egyptians and ancient Tibetan societies are believed to be descendants of the Atlanteans. It is also believed that Atlantis does exist somewhere at the bottom of the ocean and will one day rise again to share ancient knowledge with those on earth. Some say the crystals utilized by the Atlanteans and their technology still exist and are hidden to the world until the time is right for their reemergence.

Almost every household today uses crystals in some way, through televisions, watches, even telephones. Crystals continue to be an emerging source of energy.

James Tyberonn has channeled Archangel Metatron since 2007. In the hierarchy of angels, archangels are at the top, and Metatron would be at the very top. He is often mentioned in ancient Jewish mystical and esoteric writings. In the book of Genesis in the Bible, there is reference to Enoch as being ascended to God, and it is then believed that Enoch became Metatron. "And Enoch walked with God: and he was not; for God took him." Genesis 5:24. Along with the ancient Jewish writings, Metatron is mentioned often in *The Book of Knowledge: The Keys of Enoch.*

Metatron, through James, also talks at length about the law of One and the ancient souls now returning to earth to help humanity. Channeling is a known way of connecting and bringing forth information from an ascended master or other entity in the spiritual realm. A living person goes within and connects with the information or actually has his or her body merge with the other spirit. Metatron has been sending information through Tyberonn, who then shares through his extensive *Earth-Keeper Chronicles.* There is a plethora of information on spiritual development, healing energies, and the science behind the ancient sacred teachings. Tyberonn now dedicates his life to sharing spiritual and sacred scientific information received from Metatron.

Through channeling, Metatron talks through James about the fall and return of the same group of souls in Atlantis known as the law of One. He shares that these soft, highly spiritual souls are now returning to the earth to assist the earth as humanity raises its level of spirituality coming together in shared love to cocreate a new sense of peace on the earth for all. Metatron shares that "The Golden Law of One society in Atlantis represented what humanity will in time regain. The Golden Era of Atlantis in the society of the Law of One was the most evolved the highest frequency of spirituality ever achieved by humanity in duality to date." He believes these souls are here now, working toward a new spirituality on earth. Maybe some of you reading this book are part of this old soul family and are drawn to reconnect to the deep spiritual place at the center of your soul. The most important concept always stressed by Metatron and James is to only work for the highest good of all on earth. This should drive our work, love, and intentions daily.

In his book *The Lost Teachings of Atlantis*, John Peniel shares the story of his life in a monastery in Tibet with monks who were practitioners of the law of One. He spent several years studying ancient and current texts, mastering how to live what he calls Universal Consciousness. He says very real, tangible, identifiable changes can be seen in the lives of people whose consciousnesses are awakening. These are changes that everyone can relate to and are very simple. People who are becoming awakened are becoming more spiritual. It is embedded in their daily lives. Peniel writes,

> As you begin to expand your consciousness beyond yourself, you start realizing, not just believing or 'having faith', that there is more to life and the universe than meets the eye. Creation is not just haphazard. There is one great something behind it all. It pervades everything, including you, including all other people, animals, life, even the Earth and universe. As your universal or spiritual consciousness continues to grow, you start understanding the underlying connection of everything more and more, until you eventually have the realization that others are actually part of you, and you a part of them and you are all one. As your spiritual consciousness grows you also feel, and manifest, Unselfish Love, and the real world spiritual virtues that are reflections of Unselfishly Loving, like caring, kindness, compassion, giving, and harmlessness. These are the things that are truly important and the earmarks of true spirituality.

People today spend too much time on learning or having spiritual knowledge rather than simple goodness. Peniel believes and has seen that living within this simple truth can change our lives forever. It is not something that just happens. It requires conscious thought, conscious intention, and daily practice to attain.

The law of One is a spiritual way of living life, not a religion. It is based on science and the universal laws. The natural laws of the universe include the patterning and numbering of the geometry of the universe. This is the same recurring patterning and numbering within nature here on earth. The law of One is understanding and living within the life flow, the natural flow of the world. It is simple and unique, and the focus includes service to others, compassion, and love. It is a way of being one with all creation. Yet in this simplicity, it can be quite complicated. Everyone can say they believe and live these things, but the difference is in who you are, what you do, and what you think. Who you are and how you behave is the true essence of enlightenment within the law of One. On earth, humans are the only creation that tends to be out of step with the universal flow, the life force, nature, and the universe. Look around at the human suffering, starvation, greed, and lust for more money. According to the law of One, being out of sync is the cause of all of the world's problems.

The *Law of One* books, or the Ra material, was channeled by L/L Research members Carla Rueckert, Don Elkins, and Jim McCarty between 1981 and 1984. Carla Rueckert still writes and publishes on the Ra material today. The entity called Ra (not connected to the Egyptian sun god) stated in one session, "I am Ra. The Law of One, though beyond the limitations of name, as you call vibratory sound complexes, may be approximated by stating that all things are one, that there is no polarity, no right or wrong, no disharmony, but only identity. All is one, and that one is love/light, light/love, the Infinite Creator." Carla goes on to say that love, free will, and light create on their own, yet all from the One. If you see this, really understand it, and become aware, using it is a responsibility. Within this responsibility are two choices: to be of service to self or service to others. She describes service to self as energy pulled in to self for self-gain, without regard for others. Conversely, service to others is energy going outward in compassion, without thought of personal gain. Service is conscious work and requires conscious daily effort without ego. Believing in the law of One would support service to others as the one and only way to spiritual enlightenment. We are all connected in the One, so what we do to others we do to ourselves. The law of One means living and believing that doing for others is more important than serving the self. Like the Law of Attraction, this is the only real way to receive life's abundance back to you.

It should be noted here that service to others does not mean being or acting to the detriment of you. This is also a great understanding and truth. Service to others is always serving for the greater good, so it does not always mean giving in to someone else or always giving others what they want. Understanding this difference is very important, as it helps set healthy boundaries. Service to others is learning when to teach a person to fish rather than giving someone all your fish so you and your family can no longer eat. But it is either feeding or teaching someone to fish, not turning your back on an individual. Within this holds another great wisdom of free will. If someone refuses to learn to fish and simply wants to take from you, leaving that person to learn his or her own lesson of hunger is also appropriate. However, when the individual is ready, then embracing him or her with open arms and teaching the person to fish is still the right choice. Within this wisdom, the concept of tough love is also at work. Ultimately, teaching someone to fish serves the greater good. Not only might the person fish, but he or she may also teach or feed others.

Carla also describes her personal belief as a Christian. She believes that the One is Christ Consciousness. It is the original unconditional love. Being one in Christ Consciousness is expressed in this life as service to others and an attitude and philosophy of life that create unconditional love, Oneness, joy, inner peace, being nonjudgmental, forgiveness, and compassion in all moments and situations in life. Christ Consciousness is the frequency or energy of the One, and we can each attain living within this light energy, the light that we are! Edgar Cayce supported this as he spoke about the second coming of Christ not in terms of Jesus coming back to earth but that the second coming was all humanity awakening and evolving into the Christ Consciousness. The second coming would be a world that was awake, aware, and driven by the love vibration. All humanity would be living proof of service to others through love, and all of humanity would work for the highest good of all.

Ancient Eastern religions have a message similar to the law of One and the connectedness of all things and souls. The Dharma speaks about a life lived in accordance with law, or natural law. It is living the path of righteousness, the way of correct, appropriate, decent, and proper behavior, because the path to freedom and liberation is conceived in terms of causes and effects. Some think of this as karma. Very simply, wholesome, fair-minded actions always bring positive effects, and unwholesome actions lead to suffering, misery, and future retribution … the universal law of cause and effect!

> This is the sum of duty: do not do to others what would cause pain if done to you. (Hinduism, Mahabharata 5, 1517)

> Treat not others in ways that you yourself would find hurtful. (Buddha, Udana-Varga 5.18)

It would seem both of these are based on some basic principles of common sense. However, our world has become so obdurate that common sense is no longer a shared moral viewpoint. Common sense is not that common!

Judaism also has a version of the Golden Rule: "What is hateful to you, do not do to your neighbor. This is the whole Torah; all the rest is commentary" (Talmud, Shabbat 31a). However, it is Jewish mysticism and the Kabbalah that holds parallels to the law of One. The Torah speaks of visitations by angels and visions and prophetic dreams. But it is the ancient Kabbalah that whispers of an etheric world of consciousness, dimensions, and connecting with Source.

The Kabbalah is the mystery of the beginning developed from esoteric interpretations of Genesis. It holds that God encompasses all of creation, including humans, so we are also part of God. The Kabbalah lists twenty-two paths to the wisdom of God, each based on the twenty-two letters of the Hebrew alphabet. It has long been thought that grouping and chanting the letters in specific ways in specific tones opens the mind to other realms of knowledge. Most of the ancient secret writings were thought to be magical or almost sinister, because they were so secret and only taught to the most holy long ago. Like the ancient mystery schools in the days of Pythagoras or Plato, these sacred teachings were only offered to a select few. Perhaps humming or chanting certain notes, tones, and sounds activated internal gateways in a way that sent the soul into astral travel. But we get ahead of ourselves. People following the ancient Kabbalistic ways believed that actually reaching this connection with God or the wisdom would be too much for the human brain to comprehend and could drive one mad. Even today, most Jewish people do not believe that the truest of the Kabbalistic secrets are in the popular books for sale in bookstores. These secrets are considered powerful and hold ties to all creation and the universe. The writings of the Kabbalah are complex, often confusing, and speak of a universe and consciousness that are much more otherworldly than our current understanding. These writings also speak to the secrets and the origins of the universe in dimensions, energy, celestial soul minds, and a return to a nonphysical soul life. The Kabbalah has always been seen as mystical wisdom and secret enlightenment.

One of the better-known fundamental concepts of the Kabbalah is the Tree of Life. The Tree of Life is a map of the universe and our spiritual journey into existence. It shows how the life force flows within us through qualities, energy, and consciousness, including the path of our soul back to God through the descent and ascent of the soul. It speaks of a quantum world of oneness with the creator and of all life force. The Kabbalah includes the description of the spiritual planes of creation located on the Tree of Life that align with the ways God administers the existence of the universe. In essence, it says God is so transcendent that his name literally means "without end." This encompasses the idea of God's lack of boundaries in time and space. In this truest form, God is so transcendent that he cannot have any direct interaction with the universe. The tree of life then holds ten emanations, or spiritual planes, that interact and are the bridge with the universe on his behalf. These ten emanations correspond to the qualities of God. The emanations include both the masculine and feminine qualities, as the Kabbalah pays a great deal of attention to the feminine aspects of God. There is also great significance to the specific positions and order of the ten emanations on the Tree of Life itself and their interconnectedness between themselves and God.

The paths back to God refer to the journey one takes through experiences in the learning and mastery of the emanations or spiritual planes always in a specific order. They are not separate but are intimately a part of God. Yet they are in contact and connected with the universe and humanity in a way God is not. Most important, the good and evil we do in the world resonates through these qualities and affects the entire universe, up to and including God. The emanations and path shown are (1) crown, (2) wisdom, (3) understanding, (4) kindness, (5) strength, (6) beauty, (7) dominance, (8) surrender, (9) bonding, and (10) sovereignty.

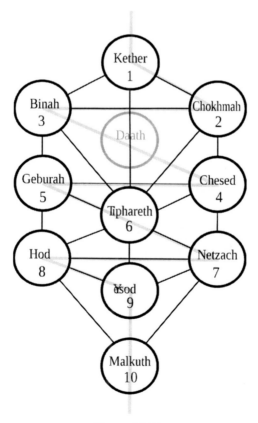

Tree of Life

In his book *Edgar Cayce and the Kabbalah*, John Van Auken, from the Association for Research and Enlightenment (ARE), talks about Cayce's insight into the Kabbalah and how it meshed clearly with the holistic oneness of all life. One concept in Cayce's teachings about the Kabbalah is the concept of "the Word," the original creation giving life to all souls. The gospel of John in the Bible says, "All things were made through this One … the Word became flesh, and lived among us." The Word, thought, or consciousness is One. Van Auken also references the mystical universe within Cayce's teachings and the ability of the mind to pass through the dimensions within one's own consciousness to actually connect with the creator in a very conscious sense. "The Kabbalah teaches that behind the visible life is a vast, invisible reality from which the visible came into being and in which the visible exists." He references that seventy-two of Cayce's readings mention the "unseen forces," which are defined in his readings as "a consciousness of that divine force that emanates in Life itself in this material plane" (Cayce reading, 281–7). Cayce believed all projected life comes from unseen influences within, not without, and all abuses in life come from the misuse of free will. The Kabbalah is steeped in the mysteries of the spiritual world within as well as our ability to tap into these mystical forces through the mind.

Rabbi Moses Cordovero, 1522–1570 CE, was a mystic sage of the ancient Kabbalah writings. He said, "The essence of divinity is found in every single thing—nothing but it exists. Since it causes every "thing" to be, no "thing" can live by anything else. It enlivens them; its existence exists in each existent. Do not attribute duality to God. Let God be solely God. If you suppose that God emanates until a certain point, and that from that point on is outside of God, you have dualized. Realize, rather, that He exists in each existent. Do not say 'This is a stone and not God.' Rather, all existence is God, and the stone is a thing pervaded by divinity." (*Everything is God: The Radical Path of Nondual Judaism*, 2009). Here we see that all of God simply is, and if we view anything here on earth as separate from God, we in essence are creating duality. God is a part of us and we a part of God. There is no separation. God does not exist somewhere separate from us.

These ancient understandings existed many thousands of years ago. Current forms of religion separate God, Great Spirit, or universal Oneness from all else, thereby creating and perpetuating a duality and separateness in our thinking. It is very important to recognize that duality focuses on seeing the difference between ourselves and others or ourselves and God. Duality does not exist other than what we create in our own minds. It keeps us from taking responsibility for our thinking and our actions, because everything and everyone is separate in duality. It perpetuates a selfish way of living for ourselves first, because all else is separate. It is the one simple way we may continue to be out of sync and weaken our connection to Source or weaken our spirituality, and we have been doing this for many thousands of years. Universal Spirit is not separate; we are not separate; there is no duality; we are all One.

Would we choose to do harm in a cruel thought, gesture, or deed if we were actually doing it to the Universal Spirit of us all? What if we were able to attach to ourselves a sharp pain that would zap us every time there was a negative thought or deed, or conversely send a flood of love and ecstasy to our heart center for all the positive thoughts and deeds we expressed? Every time you thought something cruel or did something that harmed another, a sharp pain hit your spirit first and then radiated out to your children and family before moving through your neighborhood and emanated around the world. It would be a sort of operant conditioning that might actually change things quite rapidly! Sadly, it does not support free will. Love, free will, and the right to create are our soul's freedoms here in this existence. We are all a part of the same spirit, yet we each have the free will to express that spirit any way we choose. And the free will that is expressed throughout humanity today does not always hold true integrity.

The law of One says that all things, all life, all creation stems from one original thought. This one thought is a vibration, and that vibration holds the frequency of love, the compassion for all since all are included in the one. No one can ever be separated, so there is no judgment. Our spirit simply exists as an extension of the One, and we are gifted the opportunity to be here on earth. We have this great gift to live on earth and experience all the life we can create through our mental and emotional expressions that happen from the day we are born until the day we pass. And we have the free will to choose what that looks like every single day. We are here to express and experience all life in any way we choose. Maybe spirituality is choosing love as the way to experience all life. We are all love, and love is truly all. We are unity within the law of One.

Edgar Cayce says, "Each soul in entering the material experience does so for those purposes of advancement towards that awareness of being fully conscious of the oneness with the Creative Forces" (2632–1). Oneness as a force suggests each of us is connected in ways that we might never have imagined. Our challenge is to bring that wholeness to consciousness, "awareness within each soul, imprinted in a pattern on the mind and waiting to be awakened by the will of the soul's oneness with God" (5749–14). Regardless of an individual's religion or personal beliefs, this Christ pattern exists in potential upon the very fiber of his or her being. It is the part that is in perfect accord with the creator and is simply waiting to find manifestation in one's life.

"Spirituality" defined here is a simple way of living, serving others, and doing no harm. This one simple premise, if believed by all, would radically change the world as we know it. We are the wind, the rain, the animals, and the fish. As humans we are all connected. We are each other, not defined by race or creed. Those are finite expectations put into this world, into this conscious collective, on which we struggle among ourselves for acceptance and truth. Yet all religions have one simple saying within their belief system that could begin to draw us back to the spirituality that could change our way of life and our world. It is the simple lesson we teach our children: "Do unto others as you would have done to you." We are all one. What we do to others we do to ourselves. If we are living each day, sending love to the world each day, making decisions each day, monitoring our speech and actions each day based on what is the best for the good of all, then ultimately, we are acting on what is best for us, because we are one.

We are each sparks of the creator with our own free will to build life and express that life as we choose. In our world of diversity, we are all the same according to the law of One. We all come from the same Source. The vehicle, or our bodies, that holds our spirit really makes no difference at all. Our essence, our spirit, is the same. Male or female, black or white, gay or straight, big or small, blond or brunette, green eyes or blue, we are all the same. More important, we are all one, not only part of the One, we are all one, and that one is Love. If humanity does not awaken to this huge, important, and essential understanding, our connection to spirituality and Source is weakened.

Food for Thought

Try placing the belief that we are all one in your mind daily. You are a part of Source not separate from Source. Edgar Cayce said, "The first lesson for six months should be One-One-One-One; Oneness of God, oneness of man's relation, oneness of force, oneness of time, oneness of purpose, Oneness in every effort-Oneness-Oneness" (Edgar Cayce).

Try seeing love in all things. Work toward creating a new framework by which to view the world. Consider trying to look at the world and seeing the Oneness of love, or God, or the Great Spirit, whatever name you choose to call the infinite wisdom that is the intelligence of all things within the universe. As you look at your neighbor, see yourself and see love. As you look at those different than you, see yourself and see love. As you view the earth and all living things, see yourself and see love. Therefore, as you see love in all things, you see yourself. As you put this understanding within your focus each day, it becomes a vibration. You can send out this love vibration through simple gestures of kindness and goodness every day. Try sending out this love vibration from the heart. Concentrate on seeing all things as one and sending out love to all things, as you are part of the One. This one practice alone will send love into the world.

Try practicing the ability to do no harm as you go about your daily life. Do no harm physically to others, do no harm mentally, do no harm emotionally, and do no harm spiritually to any living thing on earth. The law of One is simple: kindness and love for others before oneself. Show no harm, and do no harm to others. In its truest form, this also includes all of the world, nature, and environment as a whole. But for now, simply try doing no harm to those around you and especially those you love. This also takes a commitment to do unto others as you would have done to you.

Try being discerning of your free will every day. Each day you have many choices that face you from the moment you wake up until you go to bed at night. How do you react to the world? Actions and reactions are always a choice made daily from an array of possibilities, and you always use your free will. What is your moral compass? What are the choices you make when you think no one else really knows what you are thinking or doing? These are the choices made in a split second from your subconscious or decisions made intentionally. Just observe your awareness of what your free will is and the way you have chosen to exhibit it in the world.

Try choosing a specific time each day to contemplate your place in the divine pattern and be in a space of peace. During one of our workshops a woman spoke about her ability to stay connected in this space when she walked through her garden each morning. Another worked on this practice while walking down the beach. One gentleman talked about his contemplation happening after he intentionally changed what he listened to on his iPod while he ran in the morning. One young mother found that getting up fifteen minutes earlier each day allowed her time to commune while having her first cup of coffee before her children got up in the morning. She said this practice alone started her day in a much calmer space, before the daily chaos of family life began. Whatever time is found during the day will work. Connecting into a space of peace and love happens in your conscious mind first, before it becomes an unconscious way of life. All it takes is finding the five minutes to be present and focusing on aligning the heart and head and sending out love.

Discovering a personal sense of spirituality and identifying space daily to express that spirituality is a personal journey, and perhaps one that requires us to think deeply and trust our own hearts and minds for answers, rather than looking outward and waiting for others to help us find a way to connect with Source. We are very powerful, and our love energy, when focused and concentrated, spreads out for a mile radius. It only takes one spark of light to change darkness. Collectively we can change the world!

Spirituality is making a difference in who you are and what you do. "Those who know not that they are One, act not as One. Those who act not as One, create not Love but suffering and disharmony. What you create, you receive. The fruits of your acts will follow your days" (*The Lost Teachings of Atlantis*).

CHAPTER 3

Science, Consciousness, and the Law of One

He who experiences the unity of life sees his own
Self in all beings, and all beings in his own Self.
—Buddha

New theories are emerging from science and mathematics that challenge our views about mind and matter. These have an impact on our current understanding of consciousness. This book does not delve deeply into the sciences behind consciousness, as many renowned scientists have been observing, studying, and researching the topic in depth for many years. We only provide a broad brush of the sciences and examples of emerging research that challenge our thinking as to the possibilities of the connections between science and spirituality. The rest you can discover for yourself.

The one thing we seem to know for sure is that the universe is a lot stranger than any of us imagined. We know we are conscious beings who have many types of experiences. We experience life, emotions, nature, ourselves, and our relationships with others every day. We draw a parallel here between experience as conscious beings and our ability to cocreate. Cocreating is itself a form of experiencing our own reality as we see it, feel it, and create it. It is really about experiencing and creating our reality, our world, at the same time interconnected with each other. But what is this reality we cocreate, and what is consciousness? Do we impact each other as we cocreate? Are we all connected in some way?

There is scientific debate around the sense of consciousness existing only in our brain and a function of itself, or whether it is an energy field as an internal and external function around the human body. Is consciousness a collective energy that surrounds the body and then some? Are we ready as humans to embrace the idea that reality and science fiction may merge and that parallel dimensions can exist at the same time? Can we comprehend that we may exist in parallel dimensions simultaneously? Whether we are ready or not, physics is beginning to shed some light on all these ideas being real.

We Are One in Theory and Science

Albert Einstein was one of the most amazing scientists of our time. When he died, he left an unfinished manuscript of his latest theory. He wanted to discover the Theory of Everything. Since that time, many physicists have worked on proving Einstein's Theory of Everything exists, and they are finding some remarkable and breathtaking conclusions. It began with the study of matter. Atomic particles, they found, did not just have one location; they jumped around in random patterns, often appearing and disappearing. These particles could be in many places at one time. Through a series of experiments and building on the work of Max Planck (1858–1947), the father of quantum theory, scientists concluded matter may exist in parallel locations. These parallel locations were an astonishing breakthrough that led to the belief in parallel dimensions. The more they studied matter at its deepest levels, the more they realized something bigger was at hand. What they saw, amazingly, was that at the core of all matter, every tiny bit of ourselves and everything around us was really made up of tiny, individual strings. Each of these strings vibrated at its own frequency, with its own individual vibration or sound, if you will. In fact, they found if the string vibrated in one direction, it could be seen as one thing, and if it vibrated in another direction, it could be seen as something completely different. The process is similar to the vibration of strings on an instrument, where each note becomes its own sound. In essence, scientists realized there was no matter as such; the whole of the universe was made up of individual frequencies. These tiny bits of energy were really at the heart of all reality. This was so brilliant and simple, and it applied to the tiniest particles on the earth to the outermost reaches of the universe. Tiny strings made up everything! Scientists called this theory of all matter in the universe string theory. The goal of string theory was to unify everything into one simple way of defining all matter.

As scientists continued researching and discovering more about string theory, they found another remarkable change. After they applied eleven dimensions to the strings—which included nine spatial dimensions, one time dimension, and one gravitational dimension—another transformation happened. When they applied the eleventh gravitational dimension, the strings began to alter. Remarkably, all the strings stretched and merged into one field or membrane. All matter in the universe, all matter that makes up life as we know it on earth, became one fluid, vibrational field! The individual strings dissolved into one frequency and became one without form. Science truly supported the hypothesis that all matter exists completely within one vibrational field of existence, and it was intelligent!

Now a new theory began to emerge. M theory described how all matter merged into unity, all things were really part of this beautiful membrane field, and all were a part of one frequency. Though M theory is not yet complete, many theoretical physicists, including British cosmologist and author Stephen Hawking, believe this theory is a right step toward explaining nature on a fundamental level. While acknowledging that the understanding of mathematics and physics will never be complete, Hawking stated, "M Theory is the only candidate for a complete theory of the universe."

The Paradox of Life

In light of these breakthroughs, some scientists were beginning to look at consciousness as part of quantum physics and the quantum mind. Quantum physics or quantum theories were the overarching concepts born out of Max Planck's work around 1900. Quantum mechanics, on the other hand, was born later in the 1900s as a subset of quantum physics, because it was used to show the mechanics or field theory of the quantum world. Quantum mechanics is explained in more detail in chapter five, but briefly, it is the body of scientific research that looks at how matter behaves on a microscopic level. Yet as scientists examined the quantum world, they found matter did not behave in an ordered pattern. The quantum field was abstract and multidimensional, and when matter was observed in the quantum world, it was unpredictable and had no order. It was random at best. Indeed, this is not unlike human behavior, which is also unpredictable, not ordered, and often random!

Quantum mechanics opens the door to the kinds of things we watch in science fiction movies, complete with alternate realities, parallel dimensions, and multiple universes. It often seems the view of the quantum world is paradoxical as things, choices, and experiences may seem both right and wrong at the same time, depending on your perspective. As an example, let us say we both wanted to buy a house. From your view, standing in front of the house, it looks pristine and just perfect for your family. From my view at the back of the house, the roof is falling off, the windows are broken, and the plumbing is exposed in the walls. Both views are correct, but to me, purchasing the house is not an option. For you it is. Both views take us down different paths of making decisions. Quantum mechanics says everything in the unified field can act, become, interact, change, or evolve into any number of probabilities or realities. It is a random set of choices. In fact, you may be a builder, and the windows and plumbing can be easily repaired.

Everything in life is a choice, and every choice has its own fork in the road, which leads to another fork and yet another fork. Let us look at another example. If you choose to marry one person or take one job, your life will evolve in one way. However, if you choose to marry someone else or take a different job, your life could look quite different. Both probabilities exist. Any fork in the road we pick will have a view, a thought, and a selection before it has definition. And if I view it, my view could be completely different from your view. The paradox is that all things can be in contradiction to each other but with some sense of order. Two people may view one object, each seeing it differently, and each will make decisions based on his or her point of view. Each decision is completely different and leads to different outcomes based on our initial view. Put another way, it is only when we view something, thereby giving it a thought intention, and subsequently evaluating or measuring it that it finally has definition, which could create the decision to act.

Every situation or experience in this life happens randomly in the quantum field in our universe. It is different each time, depending on our personal perceptions. Might this be the universe providing for and allowing free will? This point of choice is the paradox of life and happens for each of us at the quantum level, of which we are all a part. Yet this one concept, as we will see, can impact the entire world and all our beliefs. Or the paradox can happen; as we know our beliefs and use our free will, the entire world can change!

We Are One in Vibration

Research now supports that on deeper levels of nature—beyond the molecular, the subatomic, and the nuclear levels, beyond all that we currently know—is a singular, universal intelligence that encompasses and truly connects all things. Dr. John Hagelin, director of the Institute of Science, Technology and Public Policy at Maharishi University, is a physicist, educator, and leading proponent of peace. He calls this universal intelligence the Unified Field or the Superstring Field. He speaks and writes extensively that as humans, we are just waves of vibration in a field of consciousness, and this connects us all together as one into the One of the Superstring Field. The Superstring Field is not created in our minds but is a single level of intelligence, and everything in the universe is included. This sounds very similar to the ancient teachings of Rabbi Moses Cordovero. If we separate ourselves from Source in our mind, taking the view that God is outside ourselves, we create a sense of duality and do not really understand that we are one. However, Hagelin brings science to a spiritual level and says that "At the basis of life's diversity is unity. It is the basis of all mind and matter, and this unity is Consciousness. It is at the core of all nature and is intelligent and we are but waves of vibration on this unified field." We are all vibration, all frequency, and all part of the One.

Hagelin also argues this field of unity is pure intelligence, pure consciousness, and transcends any one religion. It is scientific. It has been proven to exist, and we are behind the times with what is in our textbooks and what we teach in our schools. He believes this fundamental unity should be taught to our children from the beginning. It should be a way of relating to the world from our earliest learning rather than perpetuating the duality of thinking that we are all different that exists today. Children should grow up with this sense of fundamental connectedness and an appreciation that it transcends the differences between people. Schools celebrate differences in students and their cultures as a way to learn about each other, to build acceptance among all children, and to promote tolerance for each other. If we celebrate the differences between us, we celebrate the thought that we are different. Perhaps if we taught that we are all connected and all come from one Source, no matter the color of skin or what religion, we would celebrate how we are all the same, because we all share the same vibration, the same frequency. Amid all the differences on earth, we are one. If science were able to research the intelligence and emotional frequency of the one Superstring Field, they may find all are tied in love. What responsibility would we have to each other, the poor, the starving, the homeless, and the sick if they were us and we them?

Consciousness

Let us take a moment to think about the word "consciousness." Consciousness is an abstract concept we define here as including the direct thinking process of the brain. We define "subconscious" as a sort of unconscious functioning of the brain based on personal programming. Yet we also define consciousness as the holistic energy that exists around all living things as the intelligent matrix of the universe. This collective intelligence, in the world of ether and energy, impacts our lives in profound ways, as we will see. Therefore, here the holistic study of consciousness exists both as a universal collective, the entire energy field that encompasses our bodies, emits from our heart, exists among all things on earth and in the entire universe, as well as specific mental patterning or thinking.

Consciousness as a thinking function of our brains exists as a thought process that happens in the present time of now. This form of consciousness includes what we are thinking intentionally and what we are saying in words in present time. This is the thinking we can learn to observe, direct, and focus to influence our lives. But consciousness also exists as a subsection of our thoughts, emotions, actions, and words in the form of subconscious thinking. Our subconscious plays an even larger role in our world and daily life. Subconscious thought can include very concrete actions experienced in present time. We can behave from a conscious decision as well as a subconscious decision. Consciously, we could behave through some intentional reasoning and our application of free will. Subconsciously, we make decisions and behave through choices that are based on preprogramming from many sources, which we will explore. This preprogramming often impacts our behavior in more significant ways than our reasoning, conscious mind. And even more challenging, collective consciousness is a field of energy that experiences and expresses all thought and emotion by every living thing in the universe.

How much does our consciousness or subconscious thought influence our culture, or how much does our culture affect our subconscious thought and behavior? Does our subconscious or conscious thought affect our ability to hold a one-on-one connection with Source? Does Source exist in the collective consciousness of us all? We explore each of these in the following pages.

Neuroscientists and academics in places like the Center for Consciousness Studies at the University of Arizona, in Tucson research consciousness. Dr. Stuart Hameroff, an anesthesiologist from the University of Arizona, teamed with Sir Roger Penrose, a British physicist, and developed a quantum theory of consciousness called orchestrated objective reduction (Orch OR), which connects brain processes to fundamental space-time geometry. They examined consciousness as a function of reality within the quantum world, where space and time are on the same continuum. Hameroff further explored the theoretical implications of Orch, which seem to indicate consciousness can exist *independent* of the body. He believes it raises possible future scientific approaches to the study of the soul and spirituality. He talks about the future of the study of consciousness as existing between the classical and quantum worlds. Scientists and academics are working to bring a blend of research into a practical spiritual place to understand it holistically. His research also supports the collective consciousness theory.

An interesting development in the field of consciousness is the understanding of the new science of memetics, which has a definite influence both consciously and subconsciously. Memes first emerged in the 1990s as a way to view cultural evolvement as a function of consciousness. A meme is an idea, behavior, or style that spreads from person to person within a culture and becomes a new element in the conscious field of everyone in that culture. A meme can act as a unit for carrying cultural ideas, symbols, or practices and can be transmitted from one mind to another through writing, speech, rituals, and possibly music or other phenomena. It is a way that consciousness grows subconsciously or through direct conscious thought. Some believe that similar to genes, memes self-replicate, mutate, and respond to selective pressures. Linda Gabriel, in her writings in *Thought Medicine*, talks about understanding this new science and its implications on our collective consciousness, the Universal Consciousness, if you will, that can impact humanity in significant ways. She views memes through the lens of three basic concepts and how we experience consciousness.

The first lens is that our subconscious is more powerful by far than our conscious mind. The subconscious mind is usually in charge of behavior. Even driving can happen subconsciously as our minds are preoccupied with other things. Hypnotherapists can attest to working with clients and how a patient's subconscious behaviors are a significant part of the therapist's practice. Gabriel also believes that collective subconscious thinking exists in the world as a result of all we have experienced, felt, watched, read, or had fed to us subliminally through marketing, media, or other means. Consciously we control thoughts in the now. But subconsciously we exist as a result of all prior programming and beliefs and, therefore, are subjected to cultural memes as a big part of our thinking and belief systems. This becomes important when we discuss our ability to create our reality and how the subconscious can also drive that process.

Second, thoughts are seeds from which our decisions and actions grow. Everything begins with a thought. It is here that the new science of memetics emerges as memes, or units of consciousness or thoughts, interact, replicate, and evolve. Richard Dawkins coined the word "meme" in his book *The Selfish Gene*. The basic tenet is that the mind is not so much the creator of thoughts but a "carrier host" for many of them. A good or successful meme is an idea or belief that spreads easily throughout a population. It is not the same as a good idea. Dawkins states that a meme is the basic unit of cultural transmission or imitation, like Tweets and hashtags in electronic communication, which have infiltrated language and behavior in culturally significant ways.

As a collective, we behave differently based on these new memes. When introduced into consciousness, memes change behavior within a culture. A good meme can shift paradigms in others and is the internal representation of knowledge. In *Thought Medicine,*

Linda also states that Daniel Dennet shares that cognitively, a meme is a complex idea that forms a distinct, memorable unit. And Richard Brodie defines a meme as a unit of information whose existence influences events in a way that creates more copies of it in other minds. It is a way of looking at things. Brodie says, "It is looking at ideas, or memes, as distinct entities in competition for a share of your mind and a share of everyone else's. When those ideas are harmful ... understanding this model can show you how to combat the infection." Not everything programmed into our subconscious minds has our best interests at heart. Discerning the difference is the key. We have to choose the memes we want to spread as well as understand which ones have been seeded to us and affect us subconsciously. We need to be critical thinkers of the world around us.

Third, conscious reality is relative and multidimensional. The more we seem to investigate conscious reality, the more it seems there is no reality there. Movies are often helpful to building an understanding of abstract concepts. Linda Gabriel believes the movie *Inception* helps to bring the concept of memes into view, albeit in a shocking way. The premise of the movie is that the entire reality within the actors' existence happens not in the conscious mind of now but in the subconscious quantum mind, subject to all the embedded random programming that exists in our subconscious minds. In order to change reality a new idea must be deeply seeded into the subconscious mind. In the subconscious world nothing real exists at all. It is a world quite frightening, where no constants exist, and everything is random. Therefore, the ability to navigate or strategize life does not exist. Although it does not appear that our lives are completely out of our control, it is important to examine the concept of embedded random programming.

We are in control of our conscious mind that thinks in the now moment. But our thoughts exist randomly, without our awareness, unless we choose to focus on something specifically. As mentioned previously, our subconscious is the more powerful mind and drives our unconscious behavior. Our subconscious is fed packages of information about cultural norms, beliefs, and expectations, which then drives the way we act and think. Marketers are masterful at subliminally working our subconscious to purchase products, live certain ways, or even try to define what happiness may look like in our reality. Reality is, therefore, created by everything that enters our collective thinking and shapes how we behave. This will also be important as we discuss creating our own reality and contemplate whose reality we live in.

How many times a day do you stop and monitor your thinking? How many times a day can you identify the cultural memes that enter your subconscious collective? And most important, who creates these memes?

For many years, scientists have theorized that a universal energy or collective consciousness exists as a phenomenon that emanates from our bodies in an electromagnetic field and surrounds everything on earth. It is part of a quantum abstract consciousness within the entire unified field of all things. It is a consciousness that experiences every thought, emotion, and energy nuance collectively, and we are a part of it. If all thought is a vibration, and consciousness is a part of our concrete thoughts in the now moment, what is the impact of this collective field on our mental, emotional, and physical selves? Consider for a moment that if our subconscious thoughts in all prior programming, good and bad, are part of a universal collective, how might this collective energy affect us spiritually?

The Electromagnetic Field

Let us first look at the universal energy that surrounds all things, the electromagnetic field (EMF), from an environmental perspective before we consider how it might impact our personal consciousness. This section is not written to encourage a fear-based framework. Its purpose is to bring an awareness to consider the overall implication of what we create in the whole of humanity, and whether there might be new thinking about how we live as we learn to cocreate our reality. Our intentional thoughts and minds are so powerful that when we become enlightened beings and one with Source, none of these potential dangers can truly harm us.

But for now it is useful to understand the EMF and its impact on the body, mind, and spirit. The EMF is an actual physical electrical energy field around all things and people. Everything carries its own energy field, and our fields can interact in both positive and negative ways. Sometimes EMFs can actually affect the behavior or functioning of other objects in its vicinity. EMFs are everywhere in our environment, but we cannot see them. And some, unfortunately, are clearly harmful. Electromagnetic energy can be charged electrically, magnetically, or by radiation, depending on its source. The source can occur naturally, such as from people, the sun, the earth, or the ionosphere. Or they can be man-made, like EMFs from appliances, radios, or other communication devices, or through an electromagnetic pulse. Research is conducted all the time about the effects of technological devices on our body, electrically or magnetically, based on the interaction with the frequency of our personal electromagnetic field.

Scientists have also discovered our hearts and minds can generate an EMF that can interact with other nearby fields. We are concerned about the level of electric and magnetic frequencies emitted by cell phones, high-voltage electrical wires, and even microwaves. Most are low-level frequencies and have been deemed harmless. However, some can be much more harmful. For example, if an EMF is heated, you get the effects of a microwave. Many people report sensitivity to EMFs and claim a variety of health issues, including headaches; fatigue; stress; sleep disturbances; skin symptoms like prickling, burning sensations, and rashes; and muscle pains and aches. While the connection between EMFs and medical conditions has not been proven by doctors, some people feel quite debilitated by these effects.

The World Health Organization (WHO) admits that "electromagnetic fields of all frequencies represent one of the most common and fastest growing environmental influences about which anxiety and speculation are spreading. All populations are now exposed to varying degrees of EMFs, and the levels will continue to increase as technology advances." A draft study from the Environmental Protection Agency (EPA) reviewed fifty epidemiological studies and hundreds of biological studies that acknowledge low-level EMFs may increase the risk of some types of cancer. The study also stated more research was needed to understand the risks and exposure levels. It is disappointing that the results of research today also seem to end in a paradox; it may be harmful, yet it may not be harmful. It would seem to be up to us to decide for ourselves what we are willing to live with.

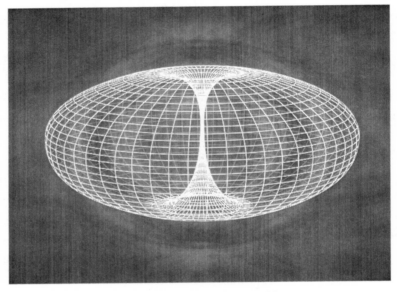

The Electromagnetic Field

Until Edison formed the first Edison Electrical Company in 1878, we were only exposed to EMFs from the sun and the earth's static magnetic field, which causes compasses to point north and animals to migrate. One article on dirty electricity published in November of 2011 discussed how scientists currently believe electrical devices throw off a sort of dirty EMF called high-frequency transients. Some of the worst offenders of these transients are microwaves, light dimmer switches, radios and clock radios, electric toothbrush handles, magnets, and fluorescent light bulbs (CFLs). We use surge protectors on our computers to protect them from transient short bursts of energy that could interfere with their function. This is important as we think of the impact on the body. Maybe we need to have surge protectors on our bodies to minimize any harmful effects.

Like a magnet, opposite charges attract, and like charges repel. This occurs in your body when you are near EMF influences. When negative transients in the home interact with our EMF, our bodies become charged as the body's positive and negative electrons dance back and forth based on the level of transient EMFs near you. Early studies showed this may interfere with the secretion of insulin and impact all the body's functions. Even more alarming, says David Stetzer, an electrical engineer and power supply expert in Blair, Wisconsin, is that in the early 1990s, as transients began overloading utility wiring, public service commissions in many states told utilities to drive neutral rods into the ground on every existing pole and every new one they erected. "Today, more than 70% of all current going out on the wires returns to substations via the earth, says Stetzer, encountering along the way all sorts of subterranean conductors, such as water, sewer, and natural-gas pipes that ferry even more electrical pollution into your home" (Prevention Magazine). Now we see that the earth is inundated with transient electricity and is also a conductor sending transient electricity back into your home.

Many people are concerned with EMF levels in their homes and the impact they may have on their bodies and minds. If your clock radio or cell phone is near your head all night, you are exposed to levels of EMFs for long periods while you sleep. Just as some people are more susceptible to allergies or have sensitivities to the environment; some people may be more affected by these EMFs than others. Questions are even being raised as to the effects EMFs may have on the mind and possible interference they may have with the meditation process and chakra fields, as the energy fields around the body are affected. Knowing how your body works will help you determine if EMFs are negatively affecting you.

In the new "smart" world, our smart phones are already connected to the electrical matrix around the earth. A new smart meter has been developed that can be mounted on homes. It is designed to measure the amount of energy used within the home. However, the amount of transient electricity the meter emits back into the home is high enough to be deemed harmful by some. Yet, it seems only a few people in the United States and the United Kingdom are protesting the mounting of these meters on their homes. Some individuals in the United States are already documenting adverse health effects from these meters. It seems the majority of Americans are either uninformed or have a high tolerance for what we will allow. As always, do your own research to discern for yourselves what you will tolerate for yourself and your family. Be informed, and decide how you can help.

The impact on living things by grounding transient electricity back into the earth from every electrical pole is not known. However, electrical transients running through the earth touch all living things. I remember a neighbor when we lived in Minnesota who contacted officials to try to resolve how electrical currents would be running through his frozen barn floor in the winter. The currents caused his cows to jump around all night long, as though they were stepping on something giving them small electrical shocks. Tests from city and government sources did not reveal any specific source of the electrical current, so the cows had to live with the fact they were constantly standing on low levels of electricity. Even more alarming are the enormous landfills full of batteries and electrical devices. There are places that recycle things like cell phones and batteries, but many harmful products still fall into landfills. This practice allows harmful chemicals and electricity to eventually seep into the earth.

Another emerging technology is transient electronics, and it looks to solve the problem of landfill pollution due to discarded older technology. Creators of transient electronics are developing devices such as cell phones, watches, and medical devices that dissolve after a "programmed" length of time, citing people's desire to upgrade technology on a continual basis as the foundation for creating these innovations. *Forbes* ran an article in September 2012 referring to a military-backed venture into transient electronics. It mentioned three scenarios: implanting devices into wounds that would dissolve over time; environmental sensors dispersed over an oil spill, sending data to earth before dissolving; and clandestine listening devices, sending recorded conversations back to military operatives and then vanishing before they can be found. The ramifications are interesting and alarming.

Another potentially harmful EMF worth mentioning is the high-altitude electromagnetic pulse, or HEMP, which presents a real danger to all humankind. It is incumbent on all of us to learn as much as we can about the nature of this threat.

> A high altitude electromagnetic pulse is a massive atmospherically conducted current of electricity that in certain circumstances would be capable of destroying every electrical power system, as well as every electric or electronic device or appliance, within range of its point of origin. The magnitude of the current involved, which is created by the interaction between masses of charged particles descending from above and our planet's natural magnetic field, would be so significant that it would overwhelm any systems or circuits that draw or transmit electricity, literally blowing them out or frying them from the inside. These HEMPs originate in the upper atmosphere, and they can strike suddenly, silently, and without warning (Navy Department Library, 2004).

Many people feel this threat would be caused by gigantic solar flares coming into the earth's atmosphere. But another potential cause of HEMP is a nuclear explosion far above the earth, though this is highly unlikely.

From a spiritual perspective, the whole idea of EMF damage poses another quandary as scientists and EMF theorists postulate the EMF field also comprises Universal Consciousness, which actually experiences all sensations, perceptions, thoughts, and emotions of every living thing in the universe. Dr. Susan Pockett, University of Auckland in New Zealand, writes on the nature of consciousness. She postulates human consciousness is actually a local, brain-generated configuration or pattern. Her hypothesis is that this brain-generated consciousness pattern is identical to other existing patterns in the EMF. The patterning of human consciousness is the same patterning in the energy field and they comingle.

Consciousness and frequency transients all may interact within the EMF, and the impact on our conscious Oneness cannot be known at this time. If our consciousness is an energy field and the transient energies infiltrate it day in and day out, is consciousness changing? If this field of consciousness is heartfelt, does it impact spirituality? Spiritually speaking, the word "consciousness" means the relationship between the mind and the world. And because we are all one, it includes Source as well. It begs consideration of how the development of electricity in the last one hundred years has impacted our minds, hearts, spirits, and emotions. Are the most basic electrical or energy systems of our world and our technology affecting our ability to connect to expanded consciousness as we struggle for enlightenment? Could the interruption in our fields keep us from living in the frequency of love each day, causing us to find it harder and harder to simply be in a peaceful state of mind? We obviously cannot live and continue to evolve without technology. But might it be time to consider alternative sources of clean and free energy to eliminate the dangers to our health and minds? There are other forms of sustainable and free energy that could be utilized worldwide and change the world for many nations and many people. This would completely alter power and electricity as we know it and is a subject for another book, another time.

The Heart and the EMF

The Institute of HeartMath is an internationally recognized nonprofit research and education organization, dedicated to helping people reduce stress, self-regulate emotions, and build resilience for healthy lives. They have a library of some of the most extensive and compelling research on the heart and its impact on emotions and consciousness. Their research in three key areas shows profound results documenting the heart's impact within the body, outside the body connected to others, and within consciousness as a whole. A study in 2004 found, "Electromagnetic fields generated by the heart permeate every cell in our bodies and may act as a synchronizing signal for the body in a manner analogous to information carried by radio waves. HeartMath focused heavily on evidence demonstrating that this energy is not only transmitted internally to the brain but it was also detectable by others within the energy's range of communication" (HeartMath, 2004).

Heart-generated EMFs are not just powerful transmitters to various places in our own bodies; they have the power to transmit and be picked up by other people. These transmissions, HeartMath found, also have the ability to influence others emotionally by increasing the frequency of love in the EMF. HeartMath found, "Clear rhythmic patterns in beat-to-beat heart rate variability were distinctly altered when different emotions were experienced. These changes in electromagnetic, sound pressure and blood pressure waves produced by cardiac rhythmic activity are 'felt' by every cell in the body, further supporting the heart's role as a global internal synchronizing signal."

So the heart can send out a signal that can enter every cell of the body and may synchronize the body's functions, as well as be affected by emotions. We already know changes in our emotions can impact internal functions. Have you ever experienced the ecstasy of true happiness and felt your entire body, including your heart, resonate with elation? Or the depths of tragedy and heartbreak that leave you barely able to breathe? What happens to the heart when the dissonance happens in the field from various environmental disruptors? Do we feel that in our cells and in our emotions, too? And how might we express this dissonance emotionally without even knowing it?

These research findings also show the heart sends out the strongest EMF produced by the body. In fact, it is sixty times greater in amplitude than brain waves measured by an EEG. This means the heart can send vibrations into the EMF even stronger than our brain waves can. We are finding the mind and meditation are not the only ways to connect to Universal Consciousness, and the heart may be the actual portal that connects our spirit to Source as the heart and mind work together.

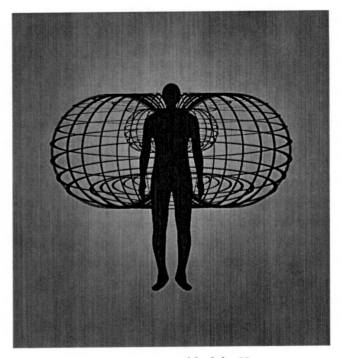

Electromagnetic Field of the Heart

In 2010 HeartMath's Dr. Stephen Morris developed a research study and found the heart was more coherent as the individual shifted to a sincerely loving or caring state. Coherence is bringing things together in a state of logical, orderly, and aesthetic relationship; it sharpens or becomes more focused. Dr. Morris was able to measure the change and impact of emotions like love, caring, and compassion. He reports, "These results suggest that a coherent energy field can be generated and/or enhanced by the intentions of small groups of participants trained to send coherence-facilitating intentions to a target receiver. This field is made more coherent with greater levels of comfort between group members. The evidence of heart rhythm synchronization across participants supports the possibility of heart-to-heart bio-communications." These results support prayer circles, healing circles, and meditation circles as truly providing an impact on focused group thought and targeted healing. HeartMath was able to measure a very different message sent out by the heart based on emotions. Our emotional heart message can impact those around us via the EMF. We are deeply connected with the earth and each other, so what we do and feel every day counts. And these actions produce EMF impulses from our hearts that have an impact on the world. The more we love, the more people around us feel that love. The more love that is felt around us, the more love is generated. It may look like a pebble dropped into a pond, as wave after wave of love converges and eventually engulfs us, as well. What we send out comes back to us.

Beyond physical ramifications, all environmental pollution in the EMF impacts the collective consciousness field in ways we may not yet know. Perhaps our current state of world chaos is caused by the inability to be coherent in ourselves, our heart to mind alignment, and our connections with others. Research suggests that groups of people can synchronize their heart rhythms, so perhaps meeting in groups to meditate together, send love out to groups, or pray together is a way to transcend some of the worldly interferences. Perhaps spirituality will include intentional focused prayer or meditation sent out to each other. Our thoughts are truly powerful, and awareness of our environmental disruptors is important to understanding what may interfere with our personal spirituality and our personal connection of coherent heart energy to Source. Focusing on clearing energy through meditation, aligning chakras, and sending love into your home and world can go a long way to alleviating negative energy.

Author and speaker Gregg Braden makes stunning observations about consciousness and the implications for humanity. He discusses these results as the potential to come together in love and prayer, and really make an impact on suffering and need. According to Braden, science was based on two false assumptions for hundreds of years. The first was that everything is separate from everything else; what happens in one place has no effect on anything else, or if it seemed to, it was probably just labeled a coincidence. The second assumption was that our thoughts, feelings, emotions, and beliefs have no effect outside our bodies. Clearly, the previously discussed research says we are all interconnected and are all one, emotionally and consciously. So Braden's identification of these two incorrect assumptions appears to be true.

Braden speaks about the data collected from the Global Coherence Monitoring System, a collaborative research project with HeartMath that measured the fluctuation in the magnetic field around the earth and in the ionosphere. The data is compelling, as it documents spikes in the EMF measured by satellites circling the earth. At one point, spikes were so dramatic that when searching for the cause for this change, the data was aligned to a calendar to discover what was happening in the world at that time. Stunningly, they found the EMF spikes happened exactly fifteen minutes after the first plane hit the World Trade Center on 9/11. Could it be that collective emotion emanating from many hearts is so powerful satellites were able to pick it up miles above the earth? Researchers theorize that when large numbers of humans respond to a global event with a common emotion, the collective response can affect the activity in the earth's EMF. What if we were living daily in global alignment with the love energy as opposed to the fear energy our media often project on us? If love is a frequency, and we worked globally every day to send out love to each other, what signals would we send out, and what would our world look like? Clearly, if we sent love to each other, we would get love back in return.

So where does this leave us, and how is spirituality connected? Science has proven all matter exists within a field in which we are all connected. Consciousness among all living things may be connected through our individual and collective EMF and quantum mind. We find that our hearts, even more than our minds, emit the highest frequency within our bodies, and there is a relationship between this field and the loving, caring emotions we send to others. We even find this field is affected as people interact, even on grand scales. Yet amid our daily lives, we are inundated with elements harmful to our EMFs within our homes and communities. Indeed, even the earth carries levels of electricity never before experienced. It has only been a little over 125 years since the first electric company was formed. And we have flooded the earth with electrical current for only twenty-five years. We have no way to know with certainty if our ability to stay in the love frequency, to hold coherence within our hearts, to connect with each other in loving ways is affected by the current state of EMFs. Yet the outpouring of emotion from every human heart affected by 9/11 could be seen from satellites orbiting earth. If our hearts are that powerful in sending transmissions, perhaps we have a responsibility to be aware of our capacity to affect ourselves, each other, and the EMF in very powerful ways. It may require a broader commitment and practice to hold our love energy collectively daily. Why would we not dedicate ourselves to the self-discipline, study, and practice to achieve this for others and for ourselves? It will take conscious effort not to be pulled into the fear mentality projected by the media and to stay focused on the love vibration no matter what happens around us. Maybe the serenity of the masters and monks who kept their course in love, no matter what was going on around them, knew their positive impact on the collective consciousness of the world.

Food for Thought

Consider taking one area of your life that you question and learn as much about it as you can. Try not to be too busy to discern what is right and wrong with the really important issues in your life, like food, water, and your health.

Critically think about what memes we internalize and what media sends to us subliminally. We function from our subconscious most of the day. Perhaps collectively we can support change!

Try keeping the heart present at the center of your daily life. The heart gives off the strongest EMF that interacts with others each day. Try a smile, a helping hand, or a kind word or gesture to expand and positively charge EMFs between yourself and others. The EMF may be thought of like the ripple created in a pond when someone drops in a pebble. That first ripple continues in wave after wave as your heart wave connects with the good works and love of another's heart wave. Put your heart into your conscious awareness every day. Keeping the heart conscious must become a habit before it will happen unconsciously.

Be conscious of things that can affect your energy field. Be discerning, and view your world through critical eyes. One simple practice is being aware of how your energy fields are affected by the environment. In order to hold the heart frequency, limit your exposure to EMFs, and perhaps consider a short meditation to focus thought and healing energy toward yourself, your family, and your home. Your heart is very powerful and can heal in amazing ways. Do your own research on environmental disruptors, and ensure you and your family use technology carefully.

Take five minutes each day to breathe. Breathing fully helps us become calm, oxygenates the blood and the brain, and has other physical benefits. Most people are shallow breathers and do not take the time to really fill their lungs. Deep breathing will also center the body in preparation for sitting calmly in meditation. Though meditation will be explained more in future chapters, here is a simple way to begin.

Sit and rest. Make your mind blank; slow your thoughts enough to catch the air to breathe in deeply, in and out and in and out. There are no tricks, tools, music, crystals, or anything else needed to connect with the divine. There is nothing more you have to do ... just be in the quiet of silence for just five minutes. Be present be in the now for just five minutes, breathing in and out, thinking of nothing. This simple time to breathe can be one of the most important things you do each day. You can do it when you first wake up in the morning, right before lunch or after lunch, even right before you go to bed at night. It matters not when you do it, simply that you do it. All you need to do is close your eyes, sit comfortably, lay the left hand cupped upon the right, and breathe deeply in through your nostrils, to your stomach from your lungs, and out again. If the mind cannot be quiet, count during each breath. Count slowly as you breathe in for eight counts ... breathe out for eight counts ... breathe in for eight counts ... and out for eight counts, and so forth. Breathe deeply, fill the lungs, and breathe all the way down the spine. Breathe with an open heart and with love. Breathe in the essence of the sun, the moon, and the stars. Breathe in the Light. Ask the collective universe to be with you and guide you along the path. Ask for clarity in whatever matter is spinning around in your head that day. It does not matter if it is work related, personal, home issues, global strife, or a healing for humanity. Just ask for clarity and send love. Stay as long as time permits. This simple step toward meditation connects you with a place within the soul that may bring peace to your heart and mind. It can also help you move stuck energies and blocks in your energy body. In time, you may begin to value this as the most important and best part of the day.

Before you read further, stop for five minutes and breathe!

CHAPTER 4

Cocreating Reality

All we are is the result of all we have thought.
—Buddha

You are where you are today where your
thoughts have brought you. You will be
tomorrow where your thoughts take you.
—James Allen

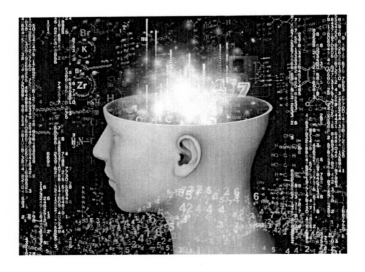

Science tells us all matter is unified at its core existence and that we are all physically and consciously united in this field. All other forms of reality stem from the basic understanding of the law of One. Once we fully appreciate that everything stems from the creation of one thought and that we all exist in this one frequency in the wave field of all that is, we begin to see the magnificence of the universe in all its individual expressions. Thought is a vibration, and as thought is breathed into existence, its only purpose is to experience and interact. We are here to experience the density of the earth plane, each other, emotion, and life. However, for many reasons, our spirits are so intensely dense in vibration that we are caught in a dual materialistic physicality on the earth plane and stuck in the dramas we create through our interactions with others. We allow our emotions to control us rather than control our emotions.

Sometimes the realities we create do not come from the love frequency in unity with Universal Spirit. Our essence, our spirit, if you will, is all part of the same consciousness, yet we exist with the ability to express this creation using our own individual free will. For the most part, our free will has not led us down a liberating path. In fact, sometimes we have not even led ourselves; we have allowed ourselves to be led by our communities, religions, cultures, media, and government. We think we are exercising our free will, but few really do. Let us consider the path of cocreation and find out why.

Basic laws of the universe, science, and mathematics influence how we manifest our personal reality on this planet. The first basic premise is that as with creation, all thoughts are things sparking from the One. The key concept is everything starts with a thought. Nothing exists without thought first. Our thoughts are projected into the realm of Oneness and take form, often grabbing onto the frequency of the thoughts of others that are like our own. We have heard and read much about the law of attraction and that we create our own reality. This idea does ultimately oversee this aspect of creation, because like begets like. However, cocreation is much deeper than our current basic understanding. Whole books are written on the concept of cocreation, the law of attraction, and how to manifest success, love, abundance, and prosperity in our lives. Many people use various methods of positive affirmations every day to change their lives and help move them into new directions. Some achieve this for themselves, and some do not. There are some definite reasons why some succeed and some don't, which we will explore.

The most difficult concept to grasp is that we are not part of a material universe that we see and feel around us daily. We are part of thought. We are a unique expression of the One, so we could say our reality is our perception of reality and is unique to us, since no one perceives it exactly as we do. Think of two people who experience the same event, and both react differently to the experience. Why does this happen? Our physical bodies each experienced the same thing, our senses each experienced the same thing, and our hearts and minds even experienced the same thing. Yet our perceptions were not the same. All we experience is fully interpreted within our thoughts. And what we experience is driven by our emotions that manifests from all our programming to that point in time. Our interpretation is not solely based on the experience alone. It is also formed by how it makes us feel and what we believe about it at the very core of our existence, our soul. That belief on a cellular level is what makes us each perceive the experience in our own way. That belief will drive our future actions, which drive our future experiences and so forth. Therein lies our perpetual creation of our own reality.

Some of us understand this process and work daily to become more enlightened in order to be in touch with who we really are in our soul. We look past the illusions we buy into in life. Some achieve that and move forward based on their beliefs and feelings. Others try and cannot seem to change their feelings about life or a particular situation, all of which are the result of their core beliefs. Their lives seem to replicate experiences, and they cannot seem to pull themselves out of their own whirlpool of life.

Though all things begin as a thought, it is important to understand there are different kinds of thoughts. There are those that program our subconscious minds and thoughts that mingle within the shared consciousness of the earth plane that construct our physical third-dimensional reality. But cocreation all begins with thought. Anything your thoughts dwell on becomes a physical reality. If you think about something happening in your life, you picture it, sense it, feel yourself in it, and see yourself in it. Eventually you will have some sort of experience along those lines. Thinking about what you want to create births the idea, dwelling on the idea begins to nurture it into existence, and eventually it will grow into reality.

It is necessary here to clarify words in your brain alone are not complete thoughts. Complete thoughts also include the beliefs you have on cellular, gut, and soul levels. What you believe in your secret heart of hearts, which you may not be able to think in your conscious brain, is really the basis for what you create in your outside world. A simplistic example of this are people who look in the mirror every day to tell themselves they are beautiful and perfect in every way. Yet deep down they believe they are too fat, not pretty enough, not smart enough, or not talented enough, whatever doubt resides inside. This would manifest a world in which being fat and not pretty or smart enough are really the underlying beliefs that drive the core experiences they receive in their lives. It does not matter how much they tell themselves something different. If they do not really believe it, their situations will never change. The example is simple but effective. We are what we think and believe.

Some have asked where fate fits in with this picture. Does everything happen for a reason? If we think back to the paradox of life, then both fate and the fact you create your own reality would be such a paradox; both are true. We do make our own choices in life, but all happens within the universal flow. It is a predestined flow of universal truth, the life force, and all happens within this flow as it should. We are presented with choices or create opportunities through thought that progress us on our path to evolve as spiritual beings. Your agreed-upon soul contract might say you have a lesson in this life to learn about something like understanding the true meaning of giving to others. You may have experiences that always seem to end up with you giving to others or feeling all you do is give, give, give and get nothing in return. Feeling you are always the giver creates situations that continually end up in dramas with others about you always giving and never receiving in some way. The reason for your continual experience of similar situations is your own focus and attention on this issue, and the emotional charge around it. You may have huge emotional blocks where this issue is concerned, and those emotional blocks have preprogrammed feelings from the last time this happened to you. This may cause you react a certain way. Even if you see a different reality for yourself, if you are not emotionally in tune with your inner being to understand giving to others first is the way to receive, your negative feelings and preprogramming will create another scenario that perpetuates your need to revisit this whole scenario, whether you want it or not. Ninety eight percent of our actions stem from subconscious thoughts, and most emotional reactions also come from the subconscious.

It is important to note the concept of "I create my own reality" does not really describe how cocreating works. We are all one, and we create our own reality along with everyone else's. Our perception of reality is viewed through the lens of all our old paradigms, emotional issues, insecurities, genetics, and experiences. Therefore, we seem to manifest into our world people with similar viewpoints and programming. We do have free will, and we can choose to view our reality in any number of ways. In fact, having free will means we have the ability to choose now something different for ourselves than what we have been receiving. But it takes understanding, observation, knowingness, and action to change the current paradigm. By choosing something different for ourselves, we bring experiences into our lives that manifest the new choices we make. We live in our individual perception of reality based on all the influences around us and those programmed within.

Before we go further, let us talk about what it means to cocreate in terms of the difference between creating and cocreating. As an individual spark of the One, we have the ability to create our own experiences, world, and expressions of life based on our past, early programming, emotions, and beliefs. Since consciousness is all connected to the One, what we create for ourselves has a connection to everyone else and to what they create. Thus, we, along with everyone else, cocreate our existence and reality.

All we build impacts every other thing on the earth. We can create from the perspective of only serving ourselves, or we can cocreate with and through service to others. We can proceed from either the I am or the we are together. It is important and necessary to address, focus, and understand the I am that I am. It is your inner being, your inner power, connected to the power of God or Universal Spirit, the Christ consciousness connected to the oneness of all things within us. It is reached through spiritual development, contemplation, and meditation and is a very personal process and experience. However, as we move into a new spiritual reality and continue working for a new sense of spirituality here on earth and a world cocreated through coherent thought sending out the love vibration into the collective, we must also understand we are moving into the we are together!

From birth, we are programmed by our cultures, family, friends, teachers, experiences, school, television, music, media, and all the other ways information gets into our subconscious mind. Some of this programming was done intentionally, and some just happened to us by osmosis. Almost everything we think and feel comes from subconscious programming. If our minds are full of someone else's programming, someone else controls our lives. The most important thing to accomplish today is to learn to separate ourselves from our self and objectively observe our actions, thoughts, and feelings. In education this is called metacognition. It is the process of thinking about our thinking. In a learning sense, metacognition encourages students to monitor how they were thinking about the learning process related to study skills and memory capabilities, and monitoring their personal learning styles. Here, this concept is so important because we learn to take responsibility for our thinking, which leads to feeling and creating actions of some kind. It is one way to begin to be responsible for the lifetime of programming that is in our brains and changing it if need be. Observe from a nonjudgmental perspective. Just stop during the day and observe the thinking. Is it positive or negative? Awareness is the first step. Just reading this book may change personal awareness, and each of us can begin to take charge of our personal reality. We always have a choice.

We are here on this planet, in this life, to create. We create with our thoughts and underlying beliefs. We create our world from the day we are born; we have no choice but to create. This can happen subconsciously, without our knowing based on preprogrammed beliefs and random daily thoughts. The result might be a foggy existence at best, driven by fear and filled with disorganization and recurring patterns of existence. Or we can be aware of how we exist in the world and how we choose to express our light as it shines out on the world. We can cocreate something wonderful for ourselves and those around us. We can be intentional about living each day and committed to doing the kinds of soul searching necessary to change the beliefs we have programmed throughout our lives, indeed, throughout our lifetimes.

Metatron, through James Tyberonn, talks at length about the law of attraction and the law of conscious creation in his *Earth-Keeper Chronicles*, saying three laws govern the concept of cocreation.

The law of attraction: Thoughts have a frequency and attract like frequencies.

The law of belief: You know beyond doubt that you can only manifest what you believe is possible.

The law of conscious creation: You have conscious ability to focally manifest objectives and events via the multidimensional mind.

He also talks about a biological reaction that happens in the brain when thoughts are aligned with belief. This alignment produces a chemical response that manifests light and vibratory frequencies within the body. Aligning thought and belief to a chemical reaction is necessary to create within the material world. We know when we are "on fire"; things are clicking, and everything is going our way. Feeling on fire or confident is actually a chemical feeling within the body that says, *All systems are go, and I believe in what I am doing.* Therefore, I believe in what I am creating and it is happening, manifesting, and being created.

Metatron also talks about doubt as a fear vibration that will creep within our thoughts when belief is not completely aligned. This doubt also commands a response that blocks the manifestation or the creation process. We all know when doubt hits us and stops our work, relationships, and personal aspirations. Doubt is a very powerful and damaging response, yet if put into the collective could draw to you others who doubt. Either others doubt you so you become your doubt, or others also doubt themselves and you commiserate.

Assumption is the unconscious key to the power of our beliefs. If we assume something, our subconscious mind accepts it as fact and proceeds to manifest it in our physical environment. Our assumptions are based on our preprogramming, current experiences, and emotions. They also affect our physical body in very real ways. Research has shown people manifest illnesses in their lives via their emotions. If we make psychological changes within the mind, we can create great physical changes within our bodies. When we manifest disease in our bodies, it is because we have already created the disease unconsciously through our thoughts and beliefs. The importance of being vigilant about the thoughts, assumptions, and beliefs that we manifest unconsciously, based on our past and current programming, cannot be overstressed.

From where do we get unconscious programming? Television is probably one of the strongest means for unconscious programming today. We are inundated with negative news and subliminal messages about how we should look, what happiness looks like, what love looks like, and what our lives should be like. There are *no* shoulds. These subliminal messages have done more to damage our society than any other means in the past hundred years. Marketers are masters at sending subliminal messages to people of all ages to sell products. But what we miss is the understanding we are left with—that negative programming and assumption turn to belief over time and completely affect our ability to create. This leads to cocreating with others who foster this same negative programming. Together, we manifest that world. As the old saying goes, "Misery loves company." Is it possible that a good portion of our world is created through negative programming and assumptions as memes within our culture?

Esther Hicks, speaker for the work of Abraham Hicks Publications, talks about cocreation and refers to the patterning in our lives and how this impacts the reality we create. She speaks about the collective consciousness as being a grid that each individual feeds and through which is then connected with all others with the same thinking patterns. Every moment of every day we decide through our decisions how to connect with the grid. We can be conscious and intentional about it, or we can slip into it subconsciously. What is the active desire we are putting out there? What is the emotional desire? She says that because we are vibrational beings, a paradox exists since there are always two vantage points. With every choice we make, either one or the other wins. Everything that happens is a paradox, and we always have a choice. Everything we come in contact with daily—from the bank teller, to e-mails, to our neighbors or work associates, or someone driving next to us in a car—becomes something our vibration interacts with that day. It is part of our grid, and the choice is ours as to what like-minded individuals we connect with at any given moment. Good or bad, negative or positive, dark or light; it is always a choice in every moment of every day. Choose intentionally, and choose wisely!

We have talked about how what you think and do can change your life in extraordinary ways. When you decide you want something, you begin to focus on it and give it energy. You can meditate on it, think about it, feel yourself in it, because it will be necessary to align your conscious mind and subconscious mind. Many times people want something or see their lives a certain way, but programming in the subconscious mind actually overrides what they want. If you have a picture in your mind of the way you want your life to be, focusing on the goal, changing old programming, learning to use personal powers of concentration to manifest it for the good of all and for you will pay off. As individuals, we need to keep analyzing and reprogramming our thinking in an attempt to prevent any new subliminal programming from impacting us. Programming comes from the media, those closest to us, things we read, and experiences we have. It happens subconsciously every day. Be vigilant about what you decide to make real in your life.

Life force is that strength you find when life lays you low and the strength you find when you must pick yourself up from the floor to move on. Life force is the strength you find to get out of bed each day when tragedy strikes. Tapping into your life force is finding the true essence of your inner self, which can be consciously or subconsciously manipulated through your internal programming.

Our ability to tap into this life force becomes more difficult when we have so many chemical blockages impeding our thinking. Chemical blockages can be caused by biological or man-made substances we put into our bodies or come from our environment. These chemicals often lower our resistance to holding coherent thought and coherent love energy. Our resistance can be compromised enough to keep our hearts and minds from penetrating through all other environmental disruptors in our lives. To truly change subconscious programming and create our best life, it is important to hold ourselves in optimal health and energy.

Our life force can heal if we choose. It is truly unfortunate that most only find this power through great adversity or illness. If we can become strong during times of illness, loss, or crises by learning to shut out all else and go within to Source in order to force through the negative assumptions and set new beliefs into motion to heal illness or overcome adversity, imagine what we could do if we learned to apply this strength to everyday life. Often it is only through great adversity that awareness comes forth, and we finally see the path clearly. Awareness must come before we consciously take steps to change our core belief system and our emotional attachments to cocreate a new reality for ourselves now.

We have seen how our beliefs control and affect the incredible powers of the mind and influence many things in our lives. Our beliefs, along with conscious choice, affect our actions, our course in life. What we create, our ability to learn and apply our knowledge can affect our choices, but it can also affect our health and whether we create sickness or wellness. We have seen that our beliefs influence cocreating our reality, and our experiences and emotions heavily influence our beliefs. Our experiences and feelings greatly influence our ability to move forward in positive thought and positive belief to manifest the abundance and prosperity we deserve and know others deserve too. The ultimate goal is to take responsibility and choose better directions for our free-will choices in our lives. Making better choices includes taking responsibility for our thoughts, walking our talk, serving the Universal Spirit of us all, serving each other, and living in Universal Consciousness. We must hold onto our thoughts of what we want in life for ourselves and others. We must maintain focus on that with all our abilities and beliefs to help us become impeccable creators and impeccable holders of the love frequency.

"Awakening" is a term used to express the soul's ability to align with the conscious mind of now. It is the first step in making changes within us and ultimately in our personal reality, which affects the universal reality around us. Physical and emotional symptoms happen to us as we begin to understand, experience, accept, and merge our thoughts with the collective consciousness. Meditation, contemplation, self-review, and prayer can combine and integrate these understandings within the heart and mind, but it requires patience and compassion to view ourselves objectively, without judgment. It takes time and experience to forgive and accept ourselves for all our perceived misgivings, and let them go at a conscious level. It also requires a strong belief in the love frequency to truly understand things we doubt about ourselves do not matter in our time on earth. Underneath it all, we are all one, and we choose to live this existence in the day-to-day choices we make in the now moment.

Awakening to a greater spiritual understanding involves being vigilant about our thoughts. We must also practice loving others more than ourselves to break away from thinking we are different or special. We are unique, not greater. Awakening also means to start taking responsibility for choosing a new path or life direction, and thinking about how our personal programming has been influenced so far in this lifetime. Awakening means being sovereign in ourselves and listening carefully to our intuition about the direction we should take in our lives. Trust and be in the vibration of love. Becoming awakened is becoming an impeccable keeper of light and love!

Food for Thought

Try strengthening your thought process. Thoughts are things. A powerful thought is an intention, a vibration, and what you send out comes back to you. People think over a billion thoughts a day. If your thoughts or the value of your thoughts shape the reality you create for yourselves, monitoring the quality of what is in your thoughts is the first important key. That reality impacts the collective reality, and your thoughts draw others' thoughts of the same value back to you, whether these are positive or negative.

Try to catch yourself thinking. It would be impossible to monitor them all, but beginning to catch yourself in what you are thinking will be the foundation of your personal awareness. Be the observer, and sit on your own shoulder for a time each day to watch what you think and how you behave through body language and gestures. You could learn much about your inner self.

Try to catch yourself speaking. Listen to what you say about yourself, what you say about others, and how you verbalize your thoughts. First, just monitor the words that come out of your mouth. This is only a fraction of the thoughts that go through your conscious mind or subconscious brain. Be aware of your verbalized thoughts at least five times a day. Catch yourself as you speak to others and begin to monitor the tenure of your words. Are they positive or negative? This also is the beginning of your awareness.

Try to learn to really believe in yourself. We have the most power over what we create when we align our thoughts and beliefs. Believing is more than just wanting something. Can you see yourself in the scenario you are thinking about? Can you add positive emotion to it? When you really believe it and see yourself in the picture you have created in your mind, you will begin to really feel it. In that feeling, a biological response is generated, and cocreation happens. So when you really think *and* believe in something ... act on it!

> One who does not learn from the past is
> destined/condemned to repeat it.
> —Law of One

Try to set an intention every day. Thoughts are so powerful they create your entire world. We can use intentional thought to impact matter when full, open, coherent energy is targeted with focused concentration. As you monitor the content of your thinking each day, you may also want to consider setting some intentional thoughts to focus on during the day. Perhaps try to create an intention every morning.

Try to frame your intention correctly. The key is asking for what you want in the right way. Make sure you are intentional and clear. The intention should always be phrased in the form of the positive outcome you hope to achieve. You can truly only affect things that impact you personally. But that impact affects others in the vibration that surrounds you. The idea is to change the *programming* that goes into your subconscious mind so that you can become more intentional about what you want to create and, thereby, purposefully influence your reality.

Try to state your intention out loud. To really be effective, you must keep the intention stated in the positive; keep the word "not" out of it. You cannot say, "I am not going to ..." Or, "I will not ..." Or. "I will no longer ..." None of these will change what you want. The universe "hears" or responds to the content or substance of a thought intention *excluding* the word "not." The universe does not discriminate between want or not want. Therefore, "I am not sick" translates to "I am sick." You have just ordered more sickness for yourself, and the universe will try its best to comply with your expressed intention. It is so important to phrase your thoughts intentionally and daily thinking always in the positive. Try saying, "I am ... I am ... I am ..." These are the things that will change you. It is also important to note that you cannot say, "I will," as that implies a future event, and the premise again shows a lack of having it now, as it does not exist now. The universe does not discriminate when the future becomes the present. Your subconscious mind is not the analytical part of your brain and cannot discern the future. It will always keep in the future what you ask for when you say, "I will." Again, the universe will always keep in the future anything you phrase as something wanted for the future. It will never manifest for you now. Instead say, I am successful at everything I do; I am active, fit, healthy and attractive; I am living in total prosperity; I am divinely guided in all I do; I am worthy of a great life; I am wealthy, abundant and prosperous; I am worthy of love and respect.

If you want to attract something into your life using your intention and powers of creation, it will have to be in the future. Yet if you state, "I want a new, white Honda Civic with gray cloth interior," you have given the intention good specificity. But you have placed it in the future. How? Because you have used the word "want." Want also implies you do not already have and generates the feeling or intention of lack. You end up getting more lack—lack of the thing you want. If you focus so much on the want, you also automatically project it as a future event. So it stays in the future and never becomes the now. In that way, your intention is always future, and future is what you get, never a manifestation into the now, the present.

The idea is to generate the feelings of having something now, even when you do not yet have it. The focus is not just on the intention but also on feelings. So the statement, with feeling, would have to change. "I love sitting in and driving my beautiful, new, white Honda." Or, "I feel fantastic driving my awesome white Honda. I love that new-car smell!" All you have to do is write a simple intention that does not include the word "want." Edgar Cayce said, "Make it real in your mind and your mind will make it so."

Try considering what you are creating for your reality. Take stock of the life you are creating for yourself. Imagine everything you have and do is exactly where you want to be. You have the job you want, the relationship you want, the money you want, the life you want. If there is something in your life you do not want, change it. Change does not happen overnight, but it will happen if you are intentional about your thinking and self-talk. Move out of thinking about what you do not have, are not, do not like, and so on. This will only keep you exactly where you are. In fact, the reason things may not have changed for you is that you keep creating the same things over and over again. It is a new creation happening again and again, because you have been focused on the same things again and again. Believe it can be different. See yourself in your new life, see yourself happy in your new life, eliminate doubt and fear, and it will come to be.

CHAPTER 5

Cocreating and Quantum Physics

Anyone who is not shocked by Quantum
theory has not understood it.
—Dr. Neils Bohr

Quantum physics is the science of possibility.
—Dr. Amit Goswami

We have discussed that all spirit emanates from the One and becomes a spark of the One here on earth. We are here to create, and we each do so based on our free will and through the lenses of our own experiences, emotions, and programming. We create our experience within the Universal Consciousness and cocreate with each other. We can each experience similar things, yet internalize it and move forward in life differently and randomly based on our human behavior and our programming to date. Our thoughts attract like thoughts as we send them into the universe, and we feed the grid of consciousness in this way. Life is very abstract, and we look to the quantum world to help us understand the multidimensionality of the universe that would allow this to occur.

We found that quantum mechanics, the subset of quantum physics, builds upon research derived from M theory, emerging after the eleventh dimension was applied to string theory and the fluid vibrational field of all matter appeared. The field happens within the quantum field. The quantum field and quantum mind are often confusing, abstract, truly fantastic, and sometimes hard to understand. Even physicists struggle with how to talk about the quantum field in ways that make sense. Science fiction movies have actually done the best job of helping us see the probabilities and possibilities of this phenomenon. If you have seen the movie *The Matrix*, you had a glimpse into the quantum field. The characters in the movie actually experience much of their lives in their minds as they sit in chairs hooked up to a machine. Even more, the group of characters actually project themselves from their own minds into a shared reality or shared consciousness. They project themselves into a collective reality through their minds as they fight between good and evil.

As we study the quantum field, projecting ourselves into another reality becomes an interesting concept. Even more interesting is the fact we have three organs with an optic center for "seeing." Two of them are our eyes. The third is the pineal gland, which helps us to imagine or see pictures in our mind. And, chapter 9 is dedicated to information on the pineal. One possibility is that the reality we see around us does not really exist at all and is completely created and experienced within our mind. Another possibility is reality is really a complete hologram, and everything we experience simply exists holographically. The study of the quantum world supports both options and more!

The nature of the universe is much different than the world we see. What is fascinating is the ultimate truth that things do not behave in any way we can understand. Quantum physics is the overarching, complete study of the subatomic realm, using theory to describe and predict various properties of the physical system. Quantum mechanics is the experimentation and observational aspect of the quantum world. The paradox is that the more we study, the more we explain about quantum physics, the less we know and the less we understand.

Consciousness and mind, objective reality, and the illusion of time are not just new age ideas. They were first discussed in the early 1900s by all the leading physicists of the time. Einstein, Bohr, Schrodinger, and others exchanged viewpoints about these philosophically, physically, and metaphysically using quantum mechanics. Some physicists continue to distance themselves from discussions around consciousness, because they still believe there are too many connections to esoteric philosophy or religion. However, when there is enough evidence that supports new thinking, if not considered we continue to miss important links to our existence in the universe.

Quantum physics studies the microscopic world based on probabilities of reality, and there is an infinite number of probabilities that make up the possibility of what is real. This is the branch of science that deals with discrete units of energy that make up everything as we know it. Even the unified waves of energy that continuously move are actually discrete particles of energy, the strings, if you will, in string theory. Early experiments trying to measure matter in the quantum field were daunting. Scientists reluctantly found they were unable to measure matter in the normal way. In fact, scientists found their actions actually influenced the investigation! They found they actually manipulated matter or the discrete units of energy, the strings, based on their expectations of what they intended to see as they measured an experiment's outcome.

In 1905 Einstein published *On the Electrodynamics of Moving Bodies*. It comprehensively became the theory of general relativity and explained the photoelectric effect, which proposed that light traveled as discrete bundles of energy. One perspective envisioned light as wavelike in nature, producing energy that traveled through space similar to ripples in water. The opposite perspective said light was composed of a steady stream of particles, like tiny droplets of water sprinkled from a garden hose nozzle. In time, after many experiments, the comprehensive answer was that both theories were correct. What was more disconcerting was that the light responded as either a particle or a wave, depending on how it was measured within the experiment. How it reacted as either a particle or a wave was not constant. The element of probability existed in that there was a certain percentage of probability that when measured as one thing, it would react completely differently.

When Einstein attended a conference to talk about his results, scientists in attendance acknowledged that as the observers, they influenced the results. The quantum world emerged, and nothing was exact in the science of quantum physics. The results of experiments could be altered by thoughts or observations. As they observed or measured energy in some way—or in a larger sense, reality—it changed based on the observers' intended results. Scientists found that if they thought particles of matter or light would behave in a certain way, they did based on the observation. So sometimes an energy particle acted like a particle, and other times it acted like a wave. When a discrete energy particle looked like a particle, it was a particle; when it looked like a wave, it was a wave. The observer had a fundamental role in determining the outcome. The wave-particle duality is the most accepted theory at the basis of quantum physics. Max Planck, Albert Einstein, and Neils Bohr discovered, and others agreed, that matter and light hold both a particle function and a wave function, depending on the aspect of the experiment, a duality if you will. In our earthbound reality, we would expect matter would always be matter, and light would always be light. On a quantum level, however, nothing behaves as we think it should. In fact, it changes as we view it or think "at" it. It changes when it is observed!

Based on this wave/particle duality, quantum physics leaves us with the unanswered and profound question, What is reality? In quantum physics, nothing is real unless it is observed. Yet scientists cannot agree on what it means to observe, because it changes the results and, therefore, changes reality. Consciousness and free will can alter the order of the probability of what occurs in an individual's reality, because both consciousness and free will can affect observation of reality. It is an old debate among scientists as they contemplate where consciousness originates and how free will fits in with current perceptions of reality.

When measuring reality, experiments showed when new information was made available to a variable in the microscopic field, the wave function of the quantum field was said to collapse and then change. When someone decided to look at energy and picked a point on the random cloud of all possibilities, reality would take a definite form. The specific point of time when the measurement occurred became the now moment, when reality was observed. So it seemed the now moment in time and the observer were both crucial to reality. What this means is that the moment we look at something, in the present time of now, it takes form and shape. We see this reality around us in present time. However, it does leave room for wondering what implications time has on our current reality. Does time or reality even exist? Does this reality exist in the future? Does all time exist concurrently? And what happens when we apply dimensions?

Classical physics, as opposed to quantum physics, does not differentiate from the now moment or the before or after. It does not include time. The observer in quantum physics pulls the now moment into view through observation, which inserts time into the equation. Including time in the relationship with reality is an interesting concept. Can time in the future affect something in the quantum system that occurred in the past? As one observes the set of random energy, it takes the form of the reality you see now. You see your reality within your own eyes and build the reality within your own mind. How do we really know that what you see is exactly what I see?

In quantum physics, reality as we know it is an illusion and changes based on what we intend it to be. Or can we say conversely that we ultimately create our own reality? We are all only energy at the core of our being. No one can predict how we will behave in any given set of circumstances, because it depends on how each of us alone perceive the situation. Might this be the probability of the observer or the concept of free will? Thus is the nature of human behavior and consciousness; there is no constant.

The Oracle ThinkQuest Projects by Students for Students identifies quantum physics as represented by five main ideas.

- Energy is not continuous but comes in small, discrete units.
- Elementary particles behave both like particles and waves.

- Movement of these particles is inherently random and impacted by observation.
- It is physically impossible to know both the position and the momentum of a particle at the same time. The more precisely one is known, the less precise the measurement of the other.
- The atomic world is nothing like the world we live in.

They further describe that while at first blush quantum physics may seem like just another strange theory, it contains many clues to the fundamental nature of the universe and is more important than relativity in the grand scheme of things.

Common Sense Science reports modern physicists do not have a single picture of the way the world really is. Instead, there are eight ideas of quantum reality. These eight worldviews of reality are quite different, but leading scientists consider all to be valid, or at least successful, in terms of explaining various experiments.

Worldviews of Prominent Physicists and Philosophers

- There is no deep reality.
- Reality is created by observation.
- Reality is an undivided wholeness.
- Reality consists of a steadily increasing number of parallel universes.
- The world obeys a nonhuman kind of reasoning.
- The world is made of ordinary objects.
- Consciousness creates reality.
- The world is twofold, consisting of potentials and actualities.

They further state the majority of leading scientists seriously believe the first worldview, that there is no deep reality and claim there is no objective reality. For them, physics is not physical but metaphysical. "All matter originates and exists in the universe by virtue of a force. We must assume behind this force is the existence of a conscious and intelligent Mind. This Mind is the matrix of all matter" (Max Planck).

We are closer to understanding the God source, or the Oneness that connects all things, when we consider the quantum field. It may be difficult for our conscious brains to understand, but intuitively, we know there is more here than meets the eye. We know deep inside there is an ocean of potential. Perhaps the only way to connect to our thoughts and observe our reality from outside the self is to quiet our mind and go within. Meditation can be the link to the heart of consciousness. Our ability to communicate may happen in a quantum field, where we may be able to link to higher states of consciousness that exist outside this dimension and into a deeper reality we do not yet see.

Brian Green, in his book and NOVA series *The Fabric of the Cosmos*, discusses the concept of the multiverse. The multiverse theory is hotly debated and uses string theory to explain the possibility that after the big bang, more universes exist in the dark matter of space. A multiverse has profound implications: duplicate universes, multiple realities, multiple yous. There may be new universes born all the time. There is a probability that we might exist on an earth elsewhere. There might be slight changes in the details of the reality, but the same earth could exist. Physics does show the reality of multiple universes does exist, and the big bang theory of creation may happen again and again out in space. There may be many more earths and many more of you. Scientists are uncomfortable with the implications this has on many religious beliefs around the world. They believe you cannot talk about things you cannot test or observe; without testing or observation, it is not science. Should we not contemplate these new discoveries in their wholeness, regardless of the implications they may have on some perceptions we have believed for thousands of years that may now be outdated? Perhaps considering other options or possibilities will help us grow and evolve.

We experience our reality through our five senses. That is how we process information so that it makes sense to us, and we can build connections and meaning in our lives. If we cannot see it, hear it, feel it, taste it, or smell it, if we cannot prove or measure it, it must not exist. But maybe it can. New information and experiences continue to change our view of the world as we learn. We change our mental model or our worldview as we experience and process new things.

Perhaps there are realms we simply cannot conceive of yet. Just because we cannot perceive something does not mean it cannot exist, and it could actually be right next to us. This may be the element of the paranormal that some believe. We recognize other universes and dimensions exist, but who is to say they do not exist concurrently within our own? Perhaps we just cannot see them. Scientists even say it is possible we exist in the same form in another universe. In this parallel universe, we might look exactly like we do, but details about our lives may be different. However, the possibility also exists there may be many more worlds and people who do not look exactly like us and do not live life as we do. This may be the element of life in the universe we continue to miss in our current reality. UFOs are still an abstract concept for many people.

In short, nothing is as it seems in the quantum world. Nothing exists as we expect it to exist, and there is no certainty that a particular reality or circumstance will act like or be like this again. The randomness of quantum physics is the foundation of our reality. There is no exact science that says we will perceive something in the same way. Many outcomes exist for how we interact with our thoughts and how we view things in our reality. Our thoughts and intentions can actually impact the energy waves or particles. If we intend and send focused, coherent thought into consciousness, the picture of that intention just may materialize!

Thought, intentional thought, can change or impact reality in surprising ways. This has already been demonstrated by Dr. Masaru Emoto and his work with the effects of human consciousness on water. Very simply, he found the patterns of frozen distilled water changed depending on the intent of conscious thought directed at the water. He also studied the effects music had on freezing water. Negative thoughts and harsh music caused water to freeze in scattered, disorganized patterns. However, loving thoughts and soothing music resulted in water freezing in beautiful crystal snowflake patterns. His research definitely showed direct thought intention changed things in the physical field of freezing water. Like the HeartMath research mentioned earlier, he showed that different emotions with intentional thought affected things in different ways.

Scientists are producing experiments that until now have only existed in science fiction. In 1998 physicists at the California Institute of Technology successfully teleported a photon, which is a tiny particle of light, through quantum entanglement. Quantum entanglement happens when two objects interact physically and become intrinsically and absolutely linked for all time. Once the two interact, a set of properties or principles exist between the two. When they become separated and something happens to one of them, the information is transmitted to the other almost instantaneously. The changes in one produce changes in the other, regardless of the physical distance between the two. Each of the individual items in the entanglement holds all the information from the entire entanglement structure. They pass information without actually touching each other. The photons in the experiment passed information, even though one was teleported elsewhere. Entanglement has far-reaching implications as to the ultimate connectedness we have to all things and how communication happens, and continues to happen, within various dimensions and time. The connection between photons is still a phenomenon that is heavily researched. Even more amazing is that the only other place this phenomenon exists is within holograms. Research like this leaves us with many more questions than answers, leaving some physicists to wonder if the entire universe is, in essence, a giant hologram.

Photon communication becomes more interesting to metaphysics when we consider the work of German biophysicist Fritz-Albert Popp, whose research shows all living cells in plants, animals, and humans emit light in the form of biophotons, which are the tiny particles of light in our cells and the ultraweak photon emissions of most biological systems. And they can be measured! Popp created an instrument that can detect and measure biophotons stored in the DNA molecules of a cell's nucleus. They also may connect cells, tissues, and organs within the body, regulating all life processes. These tiny bits of light run the gamut of the body and may serve as the main communication network, using the nervous system almost as a form of fiber-optic highway as the biophotons communicate with each other.

German physicist Marco Bischof, in his book *Biophotons—The Light in Our Cells,* found the holographic biophoton field of the brain and the nervous system may also be the basis of memory and other phenomena of consciousness. The consciousness-like coherent properties of the biophoton field indicate its possible role as an interface to the nonphysical realms of the mind, psyche, and consciousness. In other words, light in the form of photons or biophotons carry information and communicate within the body and with each other in the quantum world. And biophoton light is stored in all our cells nuclei and our DNA. Perhaps a body of light, or light body, does exist.

In another experiment to test the effect of DNA on light particles or photons, photons were placed in a test tube, and when air was removed from the tube, the photons were examined to see how they were arranged. It was discovered that they were randomly scattered. Then human DNA was introduced, and the results were amazing. The photons arranged themselves into a specific configuration in relationship to the DNA. The DNA was removed from the tube with the expectation the photons would return to their former "chaotic" state. Instead, the photons remained in the same configuration as when under DNA influence. The DNA continued to influence the photons through some form of energy communication.

In 2013 two physicists from Israel published a paper called *Entanglement between Photons that Have Never Coexisted* and actually purported to have entangled two photons that did not even exist at the same time. The photons existed within different time frames yet still entangled, sharing information between the two. Entanglement seems to happen instantly, even if the particles exist at different ends of the universe or in a different space and time. If other dimensions do exist, and we do have another universe just like this one but we live in another reality, are we connected enough to that other self to transfer information and communicate? If we each hold all of the information for the entire entanglement or possibly other forms of ourselves, perhaps a spirit self, how might we tap into this knowledge to hear it? Would it happen at the quantum level or through consciousness? Would meditation help us access it? Maybe we would not perceive of it at all, since this is a function of our third-dimensional reality based on our five senses.

Quantum particles, due to a principle called quantum superposition, exist in every theoretically possible state at the same time, and possibly within varying dimensions. A photon, which we have seen carries and communicates information in the body, spins horizontally and vertically at the same time. When you measure a quantum particle, it fixes on a single state. With entanglement, however, when you measure one half of the entangled pair, the other half instantly takes the opposite state. If you measure a vertically polarized photon, for example, its entangled partner will be horizontally polarized, sharing a form of communication. What are the possibilities and implications of such an experiment? The implications of communicating within time and space are mind-blowing. Perhaps we can communicate with our other or higher self after all. Maybe there is something to be said for our "twin flame," the other half of us as an entangled pair. Perhaps we can communicate with the etheric world as the masters suggest. The possibilities are endless. "Quantum physics has found that there is no empty space in the human cell, but it is a teeming, electric-magnetic field of possibility or potential" (Deepak Chopra).

The challenge of science at the outermost edges of our understanding is that it becomes so abstract. Though mainstream science is still not ready to talk about the edges of abstract science in terms of the metaphysical, there are clearly elements that still cannot be explained. Add to this the realm of dimensions and variations in the space–time continuum, and we wonder if we have many realities existing on many dimensions at the same time. As we discover more, we can also wonder if we have been in this reality before.

One interesting concept for consideration came from the *Lost Teachings of Atlantis* and provides another interesting way to view the potential of different forms of ourselves in the quantum realm. Multiverses may exist, but there is not necessarily another concrete earth somewhere with the same you, looking the same, liking the same things, enjoying the same music. It may be a slightly different you living within the same space–time continuum. Although the next example is simplistic and not a human example, consider water as it exists in the now moment as a fluid. But if we slightly change the molecules, it freezes into a solid. Its form is different, but it is still the same water. Change the molecules again, and it becomes steam; yet it is still the same water. In a multiverse we may coexist as an entangled entity within different forms of ourselves. What exists is your consciousness, your spirit self, your inner being, your higher self, and these may be all a part of you but exist as biophoton energy within quantum dimensions. Consider the idea that time exists as past, present, and future all at the same time, and your spirit spark, or spirit self, exists in each of them ... all connected to you now. You would exist differently in another dimension. We might even consider all the other dimensions as being more evolved than we are today.

Perhaps the spark of our spirit takes on different forms in different dimensions. Ancient teachings of Atlantis talk about the possibility that spirit exists within the One, within the One, within the One. Different dimensions, different forms maybe, different realities possibly, but all at the same time. Mathematics supports this concept with fractals, sometimes called the "thumbprint of God". What if your other selves were trying to communicate with you? Is it possible that in the meditative state, connecting to your intuition, your guides, and guardian angels may all be an attempt to contact other forms of you?

The American astronomer and astrophysicist Carl Sagan said we make our world significant by the courage of our questions and by the depth of our answers. He also believed we were "made of star stuff." As a leading cosmologist, he was masterful at bringing the cosmos to life. He noted the raw materials that constitute our physical bodies were actually, "forged in the bellies of distant and long extinguished stars." He told us we are a way for the cosmos to know itself.

Everything we know about matter dissolves; there are only relationships. We organize these relationships into holograms, which we project outside ourselves. The hologram is a metaphor here. It is how we create the paradoxes in our lives, the choices we make when we hit the fork in the road. We are all only energy at the core of our being. In the physical world, we live by what our senses can perceive. Our five senses describe everything as we know it, but science tells us our reality is only energy and not real. Individuality is truly an illusion; there is no reality. The source of illusion is within our mind. We are all one consciousness and our own imagination.

Human intention can influence the outcome of events. The human consciousness is so powerful, yet for some reason, this information is not shared with everyone everywhere. It is still the mystics, spiritualists, and a few scientists who are beginning to enlighten others to the awareness and potential of the quantum field. What is the quantum communication between the universe, stars, and atoms in our body? Is there a daily symphony? Do we have a spirit self? If we manifested this power of the conscious mind, how would it change our lives? Does the universe hear us? Our brain waves and heart connections control our physical bodies on earth and perhaps our etheric bodies spiritually. We may not exist alone if our etheric selves comingle with our physical selves or with others in the etheric realms in ways we are only still learning about.

What is clear is that to have our greatest reality here on earth, we must include each other. We all exist together in consciousness, so we must all want something better and greater than what exists today. We must all want a sense of love and peace for each other to receive it for ourselves. If we are conscious observers of the world today, we would want to bring forth something beautiful. Just watch the news to see the devastation some people have created for reality here on earth. Who wants starvation, war, and death? If the very act of observation changes things, why can we not see that as a collective, these negative actions must change? What impact do our environmental disruptors and transient electronics have on our ability to manage the energies we send and receive?

Food for Thought

Contemplate this for a minute: "Nothing real can be threatened. Nothing unreal exists. Herein lies the peace of God" (*A Course in Miracles*). Quantum physics gives us both understanding and confusion. The possibilities of various dimensions and realities are so staggering, it is difficult to wrap our heads around the implications of this science. It also demonstrates the vastness of the universe and how insignificant we all are. And yet we are still powerful beings, with the ability to alter our reality and create a new world simply by thinking, intending, and believing together.

In the worst moments of the day, recite to yourself that nothing in this reality really matters. The quantum world supports the interconnection, interdependence, and intrinsic value of all components and manifestations of life. It allows us to hope it is possible to change our reality. We can also take comfort knowing that even during our worst day, nothing in this reality is real. When you believe this, it begins to free you emotionally. By doing this distancing step, you do not have to get caught up so much in the unfolding dramas in which you participate. You begin to see things happening and think objectively about your experience as you observe your own participation. You are sitting on your shoulder as the objective observer of your life. Then ask what the experience may be offering you. What lessons are you learning from both the participation and the observation. Most important, you begin to separate yourself from the emotional dramas that tend to confuse and cloud your thinking.

What counts the most is our connection with each other. No matter what you create for your personal world, the spiritual connection to each other and to Source is all that really counts. Can you imagine being in the worst confrontation at work or a fight with your child or spouse and saying, "None of this matters; the only thing that matters is our connection, our relationship." It may be hard to see this really taking place, but in the end, it is truth.

Consider placing in your mind and belief system the awareness that there may be more to the universe than we currently know. Perhaps your spirit does connect to other realms, and perhaps other forms of your spirit exist as well. You may be entangled in the quantum world with other aspects of yourself. The field of quantum mechanics has taken research even deeper to discover evidence that supports the influence that thought has on reality. The classical laws of physics do not apply at a quantum level. But how much do we want to discover about our true nature? Our true nature is not necessarily changing how we perceive things, think about things, and interact with things in the world, because we are only immersed by our senses within our current reality. Yet if the ideas behind quantum physics are proven accurate, why would we not spend some time utilizing the science of the universe in ways that would improve our lives and the lives of the rest of humanity? Perhaps we might consider that living a more spiritually centered life is more important or takes on greater importance. Such a viewpoint may lead us to understand that assisting others to have a better life becomes very satisfying and ultimately helps us.

Take a moment to consider what drives you. What is important to you in this lifetime? This becomes your focus—what you put your energy toward, what you believe in, and what you create. Perhaps you can take a moment and define these ideas and jot them down. Is there room to consider a greater purpose that includes others in the community and a way to serve that creates a better reality for us all? If you do not like what you see, what you have written, or what you have created in your life, change it. You are in control.

CHAPTER 6

Sacred Geometry

Geometry existed before the creation.
—Plato

To truly understand the beauty of the universe and how it relates to spirituality, we have to consider the delicate balance that numbers and pattern play in the order of creation and the existence of the universe. To appreciate the uniqueness of mathematics in the cosmos, we review what is called sacred geometry, the *vesica piscis*, the simplicity of the Fibonacci sequence or the perfect numbering system in nature, as well as the incredible Mandelbrot Set and fractals, or what is sometimes called the Thumbprint of God. We also discover how these fit perfectly with the Torus, which is the core recurring pattern in the universe as a self-sustaining energy around all life. This chapter does not assume one needs to be a mathematician to understand the foundation of sacred geometry, but some explanations in mathematics are essential for understanding these concepts and their relationship to spirituality. The brilliance and order in the universe can be observed in the patterns and numbers in nature. The beauty of nature's symmetry has long been the artist's perfect canvas. We cannot talk about spirituality without recognizing our hearts and minds are intrinsically connected to the earth and all the wonders that call her home.

The belief that a supreme intelligence created the universe according to a geometric plan has origins back to ancient times. The days of the mystery schools go back to the time of King Solomon the Great. These schools have long protected the ancient wisdom of the world. Science and mathematics were revered and studied in depth as a way to know and understand the Universal Spirit. They were not taught separately, as they are today. They were studied together as a way to understand the Oneness of all things and humanity's place within the divine plan. In fact, the study of all knowledge was philosophical and encompassed all science, mathematics, and spirituality at the same time. Mathematicians, astronomers, and scientists were philosophers first and considered their science holistically. Even the builders of the day, the master craftsmen, were philosophical and considered their craft within the unity of divine Spirit. Sacred geometry was labeled as such because of the fundamental makeup of the universe and its connection to the geometric patterns and formulas used to build sacred buildings, churches, synagogues, altars, and the temples of old. This was always with spiritual devotion to the divine plan. Geometric shapes and numbers had special and hidden meanings. Much of the Masonic history lies in sacred geometry, as the original masons were the stoneworkers who planned and built the sacred buildings of the time.

The early origins of sacred geometry and ancient spiritual philosophies were translated from the Egyptian language into Greek and Latin in the city of Alexandria during the second and third centuries. A short history lesson around the knowledge held in the library of Alexandria may give some perspective on the mystical secrecy of sacred geometry. The great Egyptian city of Alexandria was an acclaimed center of learning. Alexander the Great conquered and united Persia, Greece, India, and Egypt into one vast empire. He founded the city of Alexandria but left shortly after. Alexandria eventually grew under General Ptolemy's rule and was a melting pot of knowledge and a mixture of men and women of every race and nation for many years. Greeks, Jews, Egyptians, Babylonians, Phoenicians, and even Buddhists from India lived together in peace. Alexandrians were renowned for their quest for knowledge, and the famed library and museum were founded circa 300 BCE by Ptolemy I and completed by Ptolemy II.

Over time, the library housed the wisdom of the world, holding more than an estimated five hundred thousand scrolls of knowledge. Scholars represented at Alexandria were great thinkers like Euclid, Archimedes, Ptolemy, and Eratosthenes, whose works included geometry, mathematics, geography, and understanding the cosmos. The library also housed all the esoteric knowledge from thinkers including Pythagoras (which included sacred geometry), the Chaldean oracles, Greek mythology, Platonic philosophy (or the works of Plato), the teachings of Judaism and Christianity, as well as the teachings of the Greek mystery schools, astrology, alchemy, Buddhism, and the ancient Egyptian religion from Hermes. All were studied, discussed, and debated for more than five hundred years.

The golden age of knowledge ended when the intolerant Roman Empire of the day called many of the works pagan. Reports claim a variety of events that ended the museum, of which the library was a part. It was first burned by Julius Caesar in 48 BCE, though stories conflict as to the extent of the destruction. The library seems to have another recorded loss almost three hundred years later, in about 270 CE, caused by Emperor Aurelian. Finally, the Serapeum, which housed part of the great library, was also desecrated. Eventually, Emperor Theodosius outlawed paganism, and religious conflict began in earnest. In 391 CE the Christian patriarch Theophilus followed Theodosius's lead and had all pagan temples in Alexandria destroyed or converted into churches. By the year 400 CE, Alexandria was in constant religious turmoil, and the temples were closed and burned. The end came about 415 CE, when the last great scientist and philosopher, Hypatia, a female, was dragged from her chariot by priests, arrested, had her flesh removed with scallop shells, and her remains burned. With the advent of book burnings in the temples, the thousand-year period of the Dark Ages began. The great knowledge and learning of ancient times, hidden for hundreds of years, was slowly rediscovered and is still emerging with new finds, such as the lost Dead Sea scrolls discovered within the last sixty years.

A thousand years later, in 1438 CE, the entire lost works of Plato became available, and a new Platonic academy was opened for a group of great thinkers in Florence, Italy. These men—including Michelangelo, Botticelli, Leonardo, and Raphael—began painting and sculpting, and the great Renaissance period of artwork began. Then about 1460 CE, the work of Hermes was found, and the city of Florence flourished. Thinkers were influenced at the time by the classics from ancient Greek and Roman works as well. Florence was ripe with "new learning." And as the knowledge traveled through Europe, it became one of the earliest seeds of the Protestant Reformation in Germany.

In time, the new academy in Florence was crushed by the Roman Catholic Church around 1492 CE, but the movement had already infiltrated well into Europe. New thinking permeated much of England when a young evangelist, Giordano Bruno, traveled through Europe, interpreting the new thinking as a way to unify all religions. When he returned to Italy, he was arrested by the Catholic church, tortured for eight years, and then led into Rome's Square of Flowers and ceremonially burned alive. Thus ended much of the early thinking and knowledge. But more than two hundred years later, secret groups of great thinkers, like Copernicus and Sir Isaac Newton around the early 1700s still held the spirit of the Renaissance period by passing down sacred writings, astrology, and Hermetic philosophy.

In sacred geometry, certain numbers and shapes had symbolic meanings other than just simple mathematical calculations. In fact, much was theorized and fantasized about these secret symbols as the masons continued to embed the ancient knowledge in clues in their work. For example, the mathematical equation known as the 47th proposition was attributed to both Pythagoras (sixth century BCE) and later Euclid (fourth century BCE). Yet this formulation was actually much more ancient, as can be evidenced in ancient Egyptian and Chinese architecture and the early megalith builders. These sacred numbers and shapes were already passed through secret symbols by the builders of the time. While they continue to be embedded in the works more recently, their true meaning and connection to the cosmos is still as yet unknown in mainstream knowledge.

Some basic mathematical contextual information is important for a holistic understanding of how mathematics and geometry are connected to humanity and the universe as a whole. Without getting too technical, the formulation for the 47th proposition is the sum of the square of the horizontal and the square of the perpendicular equals the square of the hypotenuse, or ($a2 + b2 = c2$). This theorem has been called the root of all geometry and the cornerstone of mathematics. It is also the symbol on the Master Mason degree and is prominent in the Scottish rite in the 20th degree. Using this formula, the architect or builder could develop elaborate plans, execute designs, and construct incredible buildings and temples beginning with a technique called squaring a room.

This theorem was also used for many other things. For example, engineers long ago tunneled through a mountain from both sides and used the proposition to ensure the two tunnels met in the center. Astronomers were able to use the 47th proposition to calculate the distance of the sun, moon, and planets as well as the length of the seasons, years, and cycles. Ancient Egyptians tied the triangle shape of the proposition to Osiris, Isis, and their son, Horus, linking one of the triangle sides to the elements salt, sulfur, and mercury; another side to the elements of earth, air, water, and fire; and finally, the third side to the five kingdoms. The five kingdoms include four commonly known materials or matter, such as mineral, plant, animal, and human. But the fifth kingdom was the Path of Return, or one who has consciously reunited with the Source. Buildings of old were carefully crafted in unison with the elements and aligned with the sun, moon, and stars. There was an ancient symmetry and oneness with nature that was included when humans constructed buildings on earth.

Mystery and intrigue spread as the Masonic Order grew in power and influence. Further fanning the flames was the development of the debated Rosicrucian movement, which emerged when free-thinkers, alchemists, and Christian Kabbalists came together to form a blend of mystical Christianity and enlightenment scholarship. Rosicrucian means "followers of the Rosy-cross." The rose was an alchemical symbol of spiritual transformation, and the cross symbolized salvation. When combined, they represented a gateway of spiritual awareness beyond the physical world. Some Rosicrucian followers eventually dissolved into Freemasons or other secret societies however there are still groups of Rosicrucians that exist today.

Some believe the Freemason movement over time was infiltrated by darker thinking, or at least elitist thinking. They believe the Illuminati, hidden deep in Freemasonry, is still the most powerful of all secret societies. Conspiracy abounds around the secret agenda of this order, including financial manipulation and world dominance, and its origins in the Rothschilds, the richest family on the planet. The Rothschilds directed Dr. Adam Weishaupt to found the Illuminati in 1776 in Munich, Germany. No one knows for sure the extent of this secret society today. The name "Illuminati" means enlightened ones. Power, money, greed, influence, and control can alter thinking when one believes he or she is more enlightened or special than another. It was believed that only a select few could have true secret knowledge, and only a few could actually connect with the divine. The Illuminati became well known through the writings of Dan Brown and his novel *The Da Vinci Code*.

Philosophers thirty-five hundred years ago contemplated nature as a way to understand the science of the earth and the connection to the divine. They considered sacred geometry in conjunction with the study of nature as they contemplated the uniqueness of honeycombs, spiderwebs, flower petals, trees, plants, and even mountains. Geometric ratios and figures can be found in most ancient Egyptian buildings, as well as medieval churches and cathedrals throughout Europe. The spiritual communities in ancient India and the Himalayas often constructed buildings around the sacred shapes and designs of the yantra and the mandala, a geometric pattern representing the universe or used in meditations that reveres the spiritual center of the design and its importance to nature and their religious beliefs.

Even Leonardo da Vinci's Vitruvian man has roots in sacred geometry. Leonardo drew the proportions of the perfect man based on the work of Vitruvius, a Roman architect whose work is the *Vitruvius in Book III the treatise De Architectura*. Leonardo, using proportions, attempted to relate man to nature. The mathematically proportioned figure of the man is drawn in the square, inside the circle. Encyclopedia Britannica online said that "Leonardo envisaged the great picture chart of the human body … as a cosmography of the microcosm." Leonardo believed the drawing and the functions within the human body were an analogy for the workings of the universe. Some interpret the work to symbolize man and his material existence, as represented by the shape of the square, and the man's spiritual existence, represented by the circle.

Sacred geometry is intrinsically linked to the Oneness of the universe, because the shapes have a symbolism linked to the creation of the universe. The word "universe" is derived from a combination of the Greek and Latin words *universum* or *univorsum*, meaning "everything rotating as one" or "everything rotated by one." In its broadest definition, it means everything—everything created and everything not yet created. Thus is the beginning of sacred geometry, which tells the story of creation in a little different way. In the beginning was the void, and the first creation was manifested in geometry. The first way for the universe to know itself was to create shape. Very simply, it began with the first shape, a single point. The single point replicated itself and then connected to become a line. The line replicated itself to become two lines that crossed each other, all in perfect symmetry and harmony. Eventually, a circle surrounded the two lines, and the sphere was born. The progression of geometry in the universe moved from the point—zero dimensional, to the line—first dimension, to the plane—second dimension, to the circle—third dimension. The circle became the sphere or space in the third dimension as we know it today. The fourth and fifth dimensions and beyond represented the dimensionality of the universe as depicted in the esoteric meanings of the geometric shapes called the Plutonic Solids.

In the universe's learning to know itself in perfect pattern, numbers and replication became the shape of a circle, with no beginning or end. Then, in infinite divine intelligent pattern, the universal expansion happened again; the circle replicated itself in unity, and the second circle was formed. The two circles represented the male and female duality. Yet the universal Source was intelligent, and within this intelligent design, both circles were perfectly proportioned with the same radius. Mathematically, the circles intersected each other in such a way that the center of each circle lay on the circumference of the other circle. The ratio of the circumference of a circle to its diameter, pi, is the original transcendental and irrational number. Pi is equal to about 3.141. The essence of the circle existed in a dimension that transcended the linear rationality it contained. Within the second dimension, the circle appears as a circle on paper. In the third dimension, it becomes a sphere with volume as we know volume to be. However, in other dimensions, the circle moves in the quantum realm, which transcends the linear rationality that we learn about in mathematics.

The place of intersection between the two circles created a shape called the sacred shape of creation, the Vesica Piscis. This is an almond shape that is created in the center of the converging circles. This was known as the beginning of life. In the earliest writings, the Universal Spirit was always represented as without beginning or end, thus the continuous circle represented God. As mentioned previously, the second circle represented the expansion of unity into the duality of the male and female. The Kabbalah and ancient Egyptian and Eastern religions all consider the center shape, the almond shape in the middle of the two circles, to be mystical, and within this shape is the seed of all life. The vesica piscis is the shape of the All Seeing Eye, found in many works of art and mathematically integrated in sacred buildings passed on through the centuries by the Freemasons. This shape has many representations, dating back to the earliest tablets found in Iraq and ancient Egyptian and Chinese art. There are many great books listed in the bibliography that go into depth regarding the symbolic meaning behind the story of creation. We will discuss several interpretations of the vesica piscis here as well.

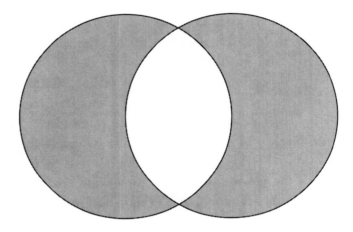

Vesica Piscis

The first interpretation of this sacred shape falls to the original joining of the male and female to create, because we are all here to create. The actual vesica piscis represents offspring, if you will. It was revered as the shape of creation because it was similar in shape to female genitalia, often seen as the symbol for fertility. As in reproduction, the circles continued to replicate. The replication of the circles also looks like what happens when a fertilized egg divides. In fact, nature uses this embryonic pattern or the egg of life, also known as the seed of life, in all reproduction on earth—no exceptions. As the sacred shape continued to replicate, it was a way for the universe to know itself, each perfectly and mathematically tied to the center of the one prior. It is believed all mathematics and all sacred geometric shapes spring from the original offspring of the vesica piscis. These shapes and interpretations predate current religion by thousands of years.

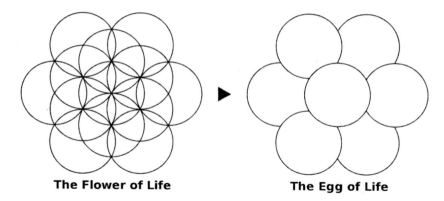

The Flower of Life   **The Egg of Life**

Seed of Life Development

The second interpretation of the shape called the vesica piscis has roots in ancient Christianity and is the symbol for Jesus Christ, which is shown today as the symbol of the fish. The almond shape of creation was considered to be the offspring of creation, the son or daughter of the creation, or Christ consciousness. As early as the first century, Christians looked for a way to continue to connect secretly with other Christians. The vesica piscis was already a recognizable symbol, and to this symbol they added the meaning of the fish. This attribution of the vesica picsis as the fish symbol for Christ was based on Christ's work, where he fed five thousand with only two fish and five loaves. Because Christians were persecuted by the Romans after the crucifixion, they used the secret symbol of the fish as a way to know one another. If two met, one would draw the upper half of the fish in the sand. And if the other person drew the bottom half, they knew they were both Christians. However, critics of the use of the fish symbol in Christianity point out the fish still carries negative connotations from the days when pagans used it to represent fertility, or more specifically, the female reproductive organs, which has roots back to the ancient symbolism of creation.

A third interpretation is depicted as enlightenment shown through art, since the shape of the vesica piscis is found as a pointed aureole in almost all medieval paintings and sculptures in churches and cathedrals in Europe. This shape was also the fundamental pattern in chapel architecture. The aureole is the radiance of light surrounding people in religious paintings and frescoes. The light either surrounds the whole figure or is depicted as a halo. This halo effect is found in churches around the Christian Godhead, the Virgin Mary, and other saints. The pointed oval is also the universal symbol of the divine feminine and is depicted on the artwork of Mother Mary, Quan Yin, Aphrodite, the Hindu goddess Kali, and the Greek nymph Phyllis.

In many cathedrals, this shape simply denotes the radiance around the heads of saints, angels, and persons of the Trinity. However, the same motif was also known several centuries earlier in pre-Christian art, where it was found in some Persian representations of kings and gods, as well as in depictions of the Buddha. Even the Egyptians have pictures with deities encircled by this sacred shape. They were sometimes depicted wearing a radiant crown or halo, perhaps portraying enlightenment. It is also interesting to note that while I was recently traveling in Meteora, Greece, and visiting the early monasteries built on the top of cliffs, the artwork inside the top of the dome of the chapel showed Christ surrounded by archangels and deities. But strikingly, the sacred geometric shape of two converging circles with the vesica piscis also figured prominently and could be seen among the other pictures with Christ and the angels. And more interesting, the entire encircled figure had wings drawn on both the masculine and feminine circles as they converged. Clearly, these monks in the 1400s had some knowledge of sacred geometry, which they held dear.

The vesica piscis also has a very powerful fourth interpretation as a source of tremendous energy. It is the original pattern, the original creation, according to the beliefs around sacred geometry. It is the central source that gives life to all creation. This interpretation is one of the most fascinating since we now have the privilege of viewing pictures from the Hubble telescope. Some of the most well-documented pictures show various nebulae in the universe. Nebulae are star-forming regions of gas, dust, and other materials that clump together to form large masses that, in turn, attract further matter.

Eventually they become massive enough to form stars. The remaining dust and cosmic materials around the star are then believed to form planets. The Hubble pictures on the NASA website are breathtaking, and there are three that clearly show the creation in sacred geometry, and the vesica piscis at the center is featured very prominently. Could this sacred shape truly be the origin of creation?

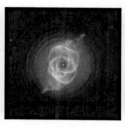
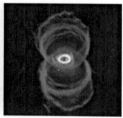

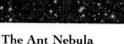

| The Ant Nebula | The Cats Eye Nebula | The Hourglass Nebula |

As the original shape, the circle, is replicated over and over, each additional circle having an identical radius intersecting the center of the circle with the circumference of another, you begin to see the symbol best known as the Flower of Life. The Flower of Life is the modern name given to a geometric figure composed of multiple evenly spaced, overlapping circles arranged so they form a flowerlike pattern with a six-fold symmetry, like a hexagon. The center of each circle lies on the circumference of six surrounding circles of the same diameter. Some consider it a symbol of sacred geometry, said to contain ancient, religious value and depicting the fundamental forms of space and time. In this sense, the Flower of Life is a visual expression of the connections life weaves through all sentient beings. It is believed to contain a type of Akashic record of basic information of all living things. The Akashic records are an energetic imprint of every thought, action, emotion, and experience that has ever occurred in time and space. The Akashic holds the records of each individual soul through its many lifetimes, creating and experiencing along the path back to Source. Leonardo described the motif of the Flower of Life as the "Egg of Life," "Fruit of Life," and "Seed of Life."

Flower of Life

The symbol represents ancient spiritual beliefs and depicts the fundamental aspect of dimensions, especially when the symbol moves from the second-dimensional view on paper and becomes third dimensional and beyond. The Flower of Life is most documented through the writings and work of Drunvalo Melchizedek, whose symbolism depicts it as the place through which light was created in the beginning. Light is the language of spirit and the communication between the soul and what lies beyond within the quantum world.

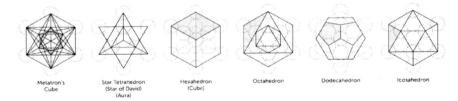

Platonic Solids

In sacred geometry, the understanding is that the universe can be explained in two ways: pattern or mathematics, and consciousness. The Flower of Life depicts how God created the universe within the first pattern of the expansion and converging circles. When the Flower of Life becomes third dimensional or beyond, and as it takes form in the quantum world, the shape becomes a sphere, and we can find all five Platonic solids within the design. These are the five main shapes that are thought to comprise every possible shape in the universe, each holding dimensional aspects of its shape connecting to the universe. These five shapes of life include the tetrahedron, cube, octahedron, dodecahedron, and the icosahedron.

As early as Euclid in 300 BCE, the ancient Greeks had a love for geometry and called these five solids the atoms of the universe. The ancient Greeks believed all physical matter is made of the atoms of the Platonic solids. They believed all matter had a mystical side, which was represented by their connection with the earth, air, fire, water, and ether. The five Platonic solids are ideal, primal models of crystal-based patterns that occur throughout the world of minerals in countless variations. In modern science, the atom shows a nucleus surrounded by electrons, orbiting and creating spheres of energy. The Greeks also believed these Platonic solids had a spherical property, where one solid fit in a sphere that fit inside another solid that fit again within another sphere. Did the ancient Greeks possibly understand the concept of fractals, or was it a further representation of nested time or perhaps the dimensionality of the universe?

The Pythagoreans knew each of these solids could be circumscribed within a sphere, and they believed the dodecahedron, having twelve regular faces, corresponded to the twelve signs of the zodiac, the symbol of the universe. The relationship between the shapes of all life is fascinating, and if one is interested in the mathematical intricacies of how these connect, there are many excellent resources for further study.

What happens when sacred geometry is expressed in the quantum world? It is thought to create Metatron's Cube, known as the ultimate shape that exists within the sacred geometric matrix. It is derived from the Flower of Life pattern and the Platonic solids, within it was thought to be the template from which all life springs. Metatron's Cube has roots in the Kabbalah as the shape that is the best known as the Chariot of Fire, or the vehicle that brings the soul to the Source through meditation. It is also known in some circles as the Star Tetrahedron, the Merkaba, or Merkana, the sacred geometry in which the spirit or the body of light ascends back to the divine. Metatron's Cube looks like two pyramids merged, one being inverted. The shape actually rotates, because all things rotate—from the galaxy to the planets, and even the atoms in your body. All things rotate in perfect direction simultaneously, creating wholeness and unity consciousness as a field of being through rotation. This field also activates the Torus, which can be explained as the regenerating energy field around your heart that unifies the field of divine perfection within. Some believe that advanced forms of meditation can utilize the Metatron's Cube and bring the soul into multidimensionality.

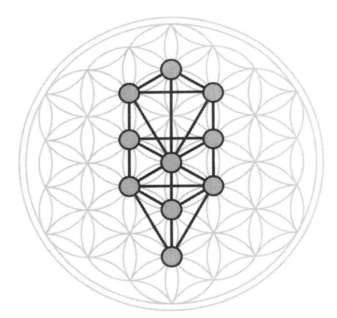

The Tree of Life within the Flower of Life

Metatron's Cube also has ties to the Tree of Life, which is often depicted as an overlay in the Flower of Life. The entire Tree of Life in the Kabbalah is a mystical framework constructed by the Hebrews as a structure for their sacred mystical pathways back to God. As mentioned earlier, it is a blueprint of the human being, and everything in the Tree of Life is a reflection of what happens within the self. The Tree of Life is the balance between the feminine and masculine aspects of God. Each idea, Sephiroth, or emanation progresses in a numerical order, with one idea naturally leading to the next and are represented in descending order. The task of the initiate is to move his or her consciousness in a process called a way to return; today some call it ascension. These qualities in deeper study are ethereal and describe how we exist and interact with Source, or the I am, our physical and spiritual selves, our consciousness, and the life force energy that flows throughout everything. This progression through the emanations is a way for an initiate to ascend back to Source through meditation practices. The levels of heaven are, in essence levels of consciousness, and we can expand our consciousness to awaken spiritually. This simplistic meaning of the Tree of Life given here would require more reading and study for a full understanding, but the purpose here is to depict that the shapes within sacred geometry have held deep spiritual meaning and connection to the ethereal realm since the beginning of time. This is ancient sacred geometry.

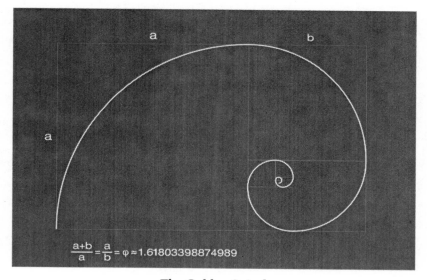

The Golden Spiral

Of note, though, are the precise calculations within the dodecahedron where the points of the sides intersect with other solids, and a pattern emerges called the Golden Spiral. It is considered sacred, and the proportion within the spiral is called the Golden Ratio. The Golden Ratio can be calculated with the vesica piscis as (X = 1.618) or phi, which appears clearly and regularly in the realm of all living things that grow. The Golden Ratio is the unique, perfect ratio, wherein the ratio of the whole to the larger portion is the same as the ratio of the larger portion to the smaller portion. Phi is the solution to the quadratic equation. It was known to the Greeks as the dividing line and mean ratio, and to the Renaissance artists as the Divine Proportion or the Golden Mean. Two things are said to be in the Golden Ratio if their ratio is the same as the ratio of their sum to their maximum. There is a geometric relationship that is expressed algebraically and said to be esthetically pleasing.

Phi can be derived through mathematics and geometry and appears in proportions in the human body, animals, plants, DNA, the solar system, art, music, and architecture. The number phi creates a spiral that keeps getting larger or smaller by the same ratio, since this pattern can go on indefinitely in either direction. As such, the created pattern is symbolically linked to each new generation, preserving the continuity of relationship as the means for retracing its lineage.

The Golden Ratio is found in the measurement of many of our human functions. For example, the sequence is found in the human body measurements of our bones, and the spiral is depicted within organs in the body, including the cochlea of the inner ear. Remarkably, this pattern is found in all of nature from seashells to flowers and more.

The vesica piscis was fundamental to the geometric description of square roots and harmonic proportions used in all of life. The square root of the first three numbers in the Fibonacci Sequence can be mathematically calculated within the shape of the vesica piscis itself. The square root is known as the formative power of polygons, because the entire polygonal world is applied within the shapes inlaid in the Flower of Life motif.

Sacred geometry is also understood today through the beauty of the mathematics of the Fibonacci Sequence. This sequence is a series of numbers where each number is the sum of each of the previous two numbers. The sequence is 1, 2, 3, 5, 8, 13, 21, 34, 55, 89, 144, and so forth. It was discovered by Leonardo Fibonacci in 1202 CE, and its ramifications and applications are endless. Sometimes called nature's numbering sequence, it is in every pattern we see around us. It can be seen as leaf arrangements in plants, patterns of petals on flowers, within the patterns of pinecones, and even the center arrangement of seeds in a sunflower. Everything in nature falls within this numbering pattern. The numbers are applicable to every single cell, grain of wheat, all nature, and humankind. It is esthetic perfection as plants, galaxies, microorganisms, crystals, and all living things are created according to this numbering rule. Even DNA is a Fibonacci sequence. And as previously stated, Fibonacci's first three numbers can be calculated mathematically within the shape of the vesica piscis. Clearly, there is an order of perfection in the universe and all living things that causes one to pause and think about our connection to the entire cosmic design.

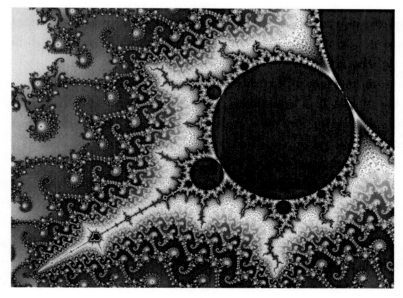

The Mandelbrot Set

Science recognizes natural patterns exist in the universe, and mathematics defines these patterns. In the seeming randomness of the natural world, we can find many instances of mathematical order involving the Fibonacci numbers themselves and the closely related Golden Spiral elements and their depiction in nature. The brain uses the same mathematics to decipher our world through our senses but seen only within our mind almost as a hologram. As we go deeper into understanding mathematics and pattern, we find this is the only way to decipher reality as we know it. "Mathematics is the language with which God has written the universe," said Galileo Galilee. Let's consider the Mandelbrot Set, discovered by Dr. Benoit Mandelbrot in 1980, while working at IBM. He brought an understanding of fractals through the art of mathematics and the help of the computer. No matter where we look in the natural world, we can find recurring patterns, and the most abundant of these are fractals. Fractals are simply the geometric result of repeating the same pattern over and over on a smaller and smaller scale, while each still holds the overarching pattern of the whole in all of its complexity. Fractals are infinite mathematical equations that are a paradox themselves. Even though they are very simple, fractals are infinitely complex. You can take a snapshot of one piece of a pattern, and it looks very much like the whole. You can subdivide the whole, zoom in and subdivide it again, zoom in and subdivide it again, and you will continue to see the same complex pattern as in the whole. It is best shown on the computer, since the zooming and subdividing create wonderful and very psychedelic looking pictures that go on to infinity. As with all sacred geometry, all is pattern, mathematics, and replication.

Nature propagates the same essence regardless of the magnitude of its expression. Perhaps our spirit can manifest aspects of its individuality on any scale as well. Nature is built on these repetitions all the way down to the subatomic level. Fractals are sometimes called the thumbprint of God, because they are the universal imprint of all repeating pattern. They are one of the most remarkable discoveries in the history of mathematics. Fractals demonstrate mathematically the duplication of a pattern within our universe, each being almost identical to the first. It can go infinitely larger and infinitely smaller and still hold the integrity of the whole. The pattern repeats mathematically over and over and over again. If all creation is pattern, and everything exists in fractals that go on to infinity, replicating the whole over and over, and pattern exists in the quantum field with the possibility of multiverses and dimensions, perhaps we go on in a spirit sense infinitely as well! Perhaps our spirit, or soul, has a definite pattern sequence that exists as a fractal and gets larger and larger and larger, as it exists on every level since the part has the pattern of the whole. Our small spark of spirit is truly the pattern of the One, the whole. Or perhaps, moving in the other direction, our spirit gets smaller and smaller, each having its own existence but still part of the whole. Maybe it is thought that exists in a sort of fractal field that repeatedly duplicates itself as it subdivides throughout the universe and beyond. If we knew our thoughts could be amplified indefinitely, would we be more vigilant about them and focus our love energy centered in Oneness in ways we are not doing now?

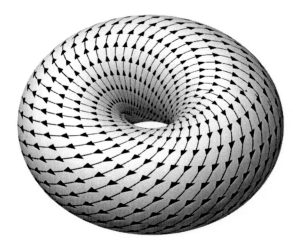

The Toroidal Field

Finally, let us consider the Torus and its impact on our spiritual universe. The Torus is a donut-shaped energy vortex that exists everywhere from atoms to galaxies and beyond. It is nature's way of creating and sustaining life. Each discrete piece of energy takes on the Torus shape to sustain itself by rotating energy. The center of the Torus uses energy that folds in upon itself, rotating so all points along its surface converge into a zero-dimensional center. This gives each point in all aspects of the Torus maximum coverage for communicating. The center point, or zero point, is the vortex. In the center, the flow of energy is in a spinning motion around an axis that moves energy to sustain itself. The energy flows around itself and reenters itself, thus continually refreshing itself. This pattern of energy movement is replicated throughout the universe, from the tiniest atoms, to all life on earth, to the spinning shape of the galaxies. It is the primary pattern used for sustaining life on all scales. In science class, you may have placed a magnet among iron shavings. The magnet automatically drew the iron shavings to the ends of the magnet, and the shape it created looked like the Toroidal field. In fact, a Toroidal field surrounds our bodies, world, and even our universe. Each Torus is unique and has the capability to energize itself at every level.

The Torus is nature's perfect way of sustaining itself and adds to the splendor and unison of the universe's exactness. Aligning with the natural flow of the stars, the sun, the moon, the precision of proportions and the numbering sequence, utilizing the natural energy of the Torus is one way to create a sense of spiritual Oneness with all life. Nicola Tesla was one of the most brilliant scientists of his time. It was generally believed he had many unrealized inventions, including a system of free electricity for the world. Nikola Tesla designed the modern Tesla coils, which created a highly magnetic Torus energy field around the coils that caused an electrical charge to jump out. What he was really working on at the turn of the twentieth century was a way to prove that an electrical current could be sent across space by using these magnetic Torus energy fields. Here is an example of how humanity may still be out of step with the natural order. Rather than developing natural sustainable energy based on nature's power for all humankind to use, Tesla was discredited and his inventions destroyed. When he died in New York City, his notes and research were lost. Instead we continued with the modern electrical company, which was developed at that time and eventually provided us with transient electricity. We have seen that transient energy may or may not harm us environmentally and biologically. Traditional electricity was a good invention but was not aligned with the natural order of the universe. If the entire world had free energy during the Industrial Revolution and was able to utilize electricity in the twentieth century, perhaps developing countries would have less suffering and look much differently now.

Dr. Nassim Haramein is one of the most brilliant physicists today. He created the nonprofit Resonance Project Foundation in 2003, which seeks to unify all sciences and philosophy. He is not afraid to bridge the science of physics with the spiritual and esoteric aspects of the universe. He often talks about the sustainable energy of the Torus as similar to atoms existing in a vacuum. And when the atoms emerge from the vacuum, they emit the information of the universe into the world. He postulates that at the very core of the vacuum, we can take one tiny amount of energy from the vacuum and power the entire earth. Sustainable energy for all may not be that far off. "When the individual experiences the holographic Oneness of the Universe, and the fundamental geometric parameters under which the life generating pulse occurs, the application of the understandings eventually generates a comprehensive technology aligned with these true natural principles" (*Thrive*).

The universe is an intelligent consciousness of sorts and not a cosmic coincidence. Spirituality just may be the physics we do not yet understand. If all things in the cosmos and all of nature, even down to the growth structure of plants, can be defined through pattern and mathematics, could not consciousness, thoughts, and emotions follow some order of perfection as well? If the life flow of energy is intelligent and self-sustaining, would we want to find some way to connect and live within the flow of nature as opposed to the current choices that create realities that do not serve humanity's best interests? How can we be selfishly concerned with our own existence and still believe we are functioning within the pristine order of the universe? Are we doing the right thing by our children as they learn—or not learn—about the geometric beauty and order of this wonderful universe where we all live together? Somewhere along the line, perhaps humanity has lost the broader, or should we say the most fundamental perspective.

Food for Thought

Try taking time to see connections in nature. There are signs everywhere. Perhaps it is time for us to consider a much larger, more complex picture of ourselves and our world and how we fit into life. We see at the very core of all life in the universe is energy, and within this energy, we are all intrinsically connected. Every living plant and animal is also part of this conscious field. At the core we find a unity of Oneness, a life force that permeates all around us. Sacred geometry reminds us of this principle of interconnectedness, inseparability, and union. It provides us with a continuous reminder of our relationship to the whole, a blueprint for the mind to the sacred foundation of all things created.

There is a system of mathematics and geometry that underlies and is integrated throughout the universe. Consider the possibility that sacred geometry and the fractal world might align to spirituality and even affect our connection to Source in some way. We are each part of collective consciousness, and when one is harmed, all are harmed. And when one is helped, all are affected! Take the time to find one area of the earth that you can help support and advocate for healing. Many people and groups exist for your consideration, and you can join others to improve the world. Consider finding a way to contribute to a cause you may not be involved with today.

Take time to spot the Golden Spiral in nature. It connects you with the profound realization that we are truly part of a divine plan. Everything is pattern and relationships, and all of this builds on an intelligent backdrop of perfect mathematics.

Try taking intentional time to commune in nature to feed your soul. Take walks, sit outside daily, hike, or even take a drive. Natural healing energy can come from taking time to smell the roses, but it is so much more than that. Your body heals as it attunes to the energies in and around you in perfect vibratory resonance with the natural world. Everything has a rhythm—the heartbeat of nature. As you become one with nature, the vibratory energy in nature aligns with your body rhythm and balances your soul.

CHAPTER 7

The Science and Art of Meditation

I said to my soul, be still and wait without hope,
for hope would be hope for the wrong thing; wait
without love, for love would be love of the wrong
thing; there is yet faith, but the faith and the love
are all in the waiting. Wait without thought, for
you are not ready for thought: So the darkness
shall be the light, and the stillness the dancing.
—T. S. Eliot

Meditation has been around for centuries. Science has recognized it as a viable technique that can impact the psychological and biological aspects of human functioning. Researchers have validated what the mystics knew; meditation can have a profound effect on the body, mind, and spirit. Meditation and the mind can heal, build concentration, and strengthen the heart's coherence with the frequency of love in significant ways. Research also shows meditation can improve physical functions in the body as well.

Meditation is the practice of quieting the mind, going within, and inducing various levels of consciousness. It can develop your ability to emanate compassion and love, or actually help you tap into the natural internal energy source or life force available through the Kundalini force or the pineal gland; both will be explained in detail. Meditation involves sitting and quieting the mind to a state of thinking of nothing. This can be difficult to do with the number of thoughts that flow through the brain each second. Anyone who practices meditation can attest to the difficulty of actually attaining blank thoughts for more than thirty seconds at a time, if that. The ability to sustain a single point of concentration actually takes time to nurture and develop. Most practitioners find it much easier to concentrate on their breathing and actually count breaths as a technique to keep thoughts focused on one point of concentration. There is no rule as to what you must do. Just practice daily, and you will improve the method you choose to practice. There is also merit in using tone in meditation, such as the Om sound, which can also help you sustain one point of concentration. Simply speak or sing the word "Om" and hold the note as long as you can. You can repeat this as often as you are comfortable. Meditation always involves some manner of self-regulating the brain to achieve a sense of focus and concentration.

Meditation can help you to elicit answers to questions from your inner self, relax peacefully, and improve your ability to continue with a sense of calmness throughout the day. Or it can help you achieve a higher state of consciousness, a theta state or frequency.

History of Meditation in the United States

The practice of meditation has been growing in the United States for many years. The meditation movement came West with Eastern yogis and teachers in the early 1900s. Paramahansa Yogananda (1893–1952), author of *Autobiography of a Yogi*, lived and taught in the West for thirty years. He brought Kriya yogic techniques and the Self Realization Fellowship that continues throughout the United States and world today. He is best known for introducing the Western world to Kriya yoga, which is a practice of directing life force energy through a number of levels, up and down specific energy centers along the spine, which rapidly increases spiritual development. Yogananda also stood for the underlying unity of all religions and balanced health in mind, body, and spirit. He believed meditation was a way to unlock the soul's potential. He taught a system of powerful meditations as part of the Kriya yoga science. Due to his influence, there are Self Realization Temples throughout many large cities in the United States, including the Self Realization Retreat and Temple in Encinitas, California.

The largest movement by far is the Transcendental Meditation (TM) movement, brought forward by Maharishi Mahesh Yogi. TM was first taught in India in the 1950s and then brought to America in the early 1970s. It is now purported to have more than five million followers worldwide. The movement has assets of over $3 billion and includes meditation teaching centers, schools, universities, health centers, and a line of herbal supplements. It has been called a social movement, a guru movement, a religion, and a cult. But TM does not call itself a religion and does not require any specific belief system. In fact, people from many diverse groups of religions and affiliations practice TM.

TM is a specific technique based on the ancient Vedic Hindu tradition of enlightenment from India. It is a specific mantra meditation practiced for fifteen to twenty minutes twice a day while sitting with your eyes closed. A mantra in Sanskrit means liberating the mind or consciousness and involves using a sound or group of words while mediating. The mantra usually begins with the Om or Aum sound, which is the most recognized sound associated with meditation. TM also teaches advanced forms of meditation that include Yogic flying. "Yogic flying leads to the body lifting in short hops from the ground. Students describe the experience of this technique as one of happiness, energy, bliss, and inner freedom, with these qualities carrying over into their daily life" (Transcendental Meditation Organization). Research shows there is a marked increase in brain wave coherence that coincides with the body lifting during this practice.

TM has probably been the most researched form of meditation for years, beginning with articles published by UCLA, Harvard, and in the *American Journal of Physiology* in the early 1970s. By 2004 the US government had given more than $20 million to Maharishi International University in Fairfield, Iowa, to study the effects of meditation on health. There are more than 350 research studies from over 250 different institutions and medical schools over the past forty years on the effects of meditation on health.

Maharishi International University was first established in Iowa in 1974, after it acquired the bankrupt Parsons College. It became Maharishi University of Management in 1995 and remains a nonprofit university that features a "consciousness-based education," which includes TM practice. It is accredited and offers BA, MA, and PhD programs with an interesting holistic approach. The university is only mentioned here because it specifically offers a holistic approach through meditation. It is only one respected institution of higher education—public and private, religious or otherwise—that choose to emphasize mind, body, and spirit through internal spiritual practice.

TM, Self Realization Fellowship, and even community yoga programs can offer instruction in specific meditative techniques and fellowship for a beginner as a way to learn to achieve various levels of consciousness. However, as we develop a new sense of spirituality, it is not necessary to belong to or follow any specific group or movement to take advantage of meditation's benefits. In some cases, that may be a distraction to true practice. It is only necessary that you do it for yourself, because meditation is a very personal journey. TM and Self Realization Fellowship are mentioned here as examples of the breadth and depth meditation has as a credible holistic influence in our lives.

Breathing and Meditation

The first important step in learning to meditate is to learn advanced breathing techniques that can help you achieve deeper levels of meditation and higher levels of consciousness. Concentrated breathing is a way to train your mind to remain on task and to concentrate with intention. When you first begin, you can control the rate of the inhale and exhale by breathing in for eight counts and breathing out for eight counts. You can speed it up or slow it as you need. Listen to yourself and personalize the experience. With practice, you will be able to balance the same amount of time you expend for the inhale and exhale. Remember it is important to always breathe all the way down to your diaphragm. You are oxygenating the body. Also important is to breathe through your nose. An advanced breathing technique could incorporate an outbreath, with a rapid pah sound, but that it something you can develop later. Just breathe in and out through the nose as a way to begin when learning.

Most people breathe from their shoulders or are considered shallow breathers as they go about their day. Shallow breathing is harmful to the body, because you need oxygen to feed the blood that runs through your vital organs. To really oxygenate the body and gain the most for the brain and meditative states, breathing should be accessed in two ways. First, simply breathe through the diaphragm. Like singing, you should be able to see the diaphragm move in and out as you breathe. Practice using this type of breathing most of the day.

A more advanced breathing technique is breathing from the diaphragm and lungs together, including both the top and bottom portion of the lungs in unison. Picture your whole upper body rising and falling together in the breath. Watch it rise and fall in rhythm, in balance. In essence, you are taking in oxygen and carrying it from the throat chakra all the way down to the sacral chakra. Though the chakras will be explored in detail in the next chapter, practice breathing, and picture yourself oxygenating each of four chakra areas along the spine every time you breathe. These are the throat, heart, solar plexus, and sacral chakras, and all are being fed each time you breathe. The oxygen is then carried throughout the rest of the body.

Many people who exercise use specific breathing techniques to keep them in an aerobic state of exertion. This balanced breathing technique is similar to meditation. In fact, paying attention to your breath while you are walking briskly can help you learn to balance breathing, counting the in-breath and the out-breath, as well as breathing from the diaphragm and lungs together. Make a conscious effort to do this regularly, and it will eventually become regular breathing.

Basic Brain Waves

Your brain is made up of billions of brain cells called neurons. They use electricity to communicate with each other. All these neurons sending signals at once produces an enormous volume of electrical activity in the brain. This combination of electrical activity is commonly known as brain wave pattern because of its cyclic, wavelike nature. Before we consider types and forms of meditation, it might be helpful to understand the brain actually achieves various basic brain wave states that affect consciousness. Brain research grew when German psychiatrist Hans Berger invented the electroencephalogram (EEG) that measures brain waves in hertz, which can be detected using sensitive medical equipment measuring electricity levels or frequencies over areas of the scalp. Over the years, more sensitive equipment has brought us closer to figuring out exactly what brain waves represent and, with that, what they mean about a person's health and state of mind.

With the discovery of brain waves came the discovery that electrical activity in the brain will change depending on what the person is doing. For instance, a sleeping person's brain waves are vastly different than those of someone who is wide-awake. The slower the frequency of your brain waves, the more relaxed you feel in general.

Gamma waves exist in the 27-hertz range and higher. Gamma is associated with creativity, the formation of ideas, language and memory processing, and various types of learning. Gamma brain waves are the fastest brain wave frequency. They bring feelings of being in the zone, bliss, or that you can do anything. Gamma brain waves are known as peak concentration and extremely high levels of cognitive functioning. Neuroscientists believe gamma waves are able to link information from all parts of the brain.

Beta waves exist in about 13 to 30-hertz, when your brain is alert and active, and when you are wide-awake. Your brain is in beta as you read this book or concentrate on learning something new. Most people are in beta most of the day. Believe it or not, many people lack the opportunity for sufficient beta activity, which can cause mental or emotional disorders such as depression, attention deficit disorder, and insomnia. Stimulating beta activity can improve emotional stability, energy levels, attentiveness, and concentration. Beta waves can also be associated with stress, worry, and perpetual thoughts running around in your head. Beta activity is alert consciousness and Beta is the conscious state we can objectively observe and direct.

Alpha waves exist in the 8 to 13-hertz range and are associated with being relaxed, daydreaming, and having a sort of detached awareness. Alpha is awake but not processing much new information. People may be in the alpha state while watching television or being a passive receiver. You can induce the alpha state by closing your eyes and taking slow, deep breaths. You begin to feel a light-headed, relaxed state. The alpha state can be so relaxing you can fall asleep while passively receiving information. This brain wave may also be a link between the subconscious and conscious mind. Alpha is a necessary state but not necessarily all day. It is important to find time away from the television to engage the brain. Medication can also cause one to be in alpha more than the beta range for most of the day. As you drift off to sleep or move into guided imagery, your brain produces alpha waves. People generally move into alpha while resting, relaxing, or when they first get up or first go to bed at night. Alpha is often the beginning phase of meditation.

Theta waves exist in the 4 to 8-hertz range and are associated with deep states of meditation, higher states of consciousness, and profound spiritual experiences. Some believe the theta state is deeply subconscious, and where suppressed, emotions and incredible creativity exists. Theta is also where dreams occur during the rapid eye movement (REM) sleep. Perhaps a theta state helps enter a sort of quantum world through meditation. Others believe the soul actually travels outside the body during times of deep sleep. Meditation is a way of taking theta from the subconscious world to a conscious one, if you will. A theta state can also be used during hypnosis or self-programming through prerecorded suggestions. Tapping into your genius may also be found at this level.

Delta waves exist up to 4 hertz and engage the brain during deep, dreamless sleep. Sleep deprivation and alcohol can interfere with sleep in delta. The importance of deep sleep is well documented by many harmful effects attributed to sleep deficiency. When the dominant brain wave is in delta, your body heals itself and resets its internal clocks. You do not dream in this state and are completely unconscious. However, meditation can help relax the body and may bring rest to the mind to induce the delta level of sleep. Some consider delta to be the bridge to what Carl Jung described as the "collective unconscious."

The measurement of brain waves in meditation is a relatively recent development as scientists discover how this ancient practice reduces stress, increases feelings of well-being, and enhances overall health. Brain waves in meditation shift through the various stages. The most common state for beginning meditation falls within the alpha wave range. In this state, we can experience calmness in the autonomic nervous system while it lowers blood pressure and heart rate, as well as the amount of stress hormones in the body. One of the stress hormones, cortisol, has been shown to encourage weight gain when elevated over the long term. Many people channel their stress into their heart, which can cause abnormal heart rhythms and clotting in the heart. Meditation can help alleviate stress buildup over time.

Theta brain waves in meditation are said to help open the "third eye." This is where practitioners gain illumination and can experience shamanic journeys or find wisdom through vibrations received through the pineal gland, often referred to as the third eye. Theta brain waves can invoke a deep sense of relaxation, encourage creativity, and enhance problem solving. Some serious practitioners of meditation believe the theta realm is where the spiritual connections to Source occur and where we can most affect our enlightenment, establish connections to other dimensions, or connect with our higher selves.

Types of Meditation

Meditation can help you achieve balance and focus your day. It can be a formal practice that includes sitting in a certain way, holding your hands in a certain way, breathing a certain way, and listening to certain music. However, some find these procedures too burdensome, and eventually this kind of structure in meditation can lead to excuses that may prevent you from engaging in a regular routine or daily practice.

Start simply. Just sit or lie anywhere you are comfortable. Close your eyes, and center your focus on the third eye inside your forehead. Simply begin breathing. After a minute or so, begin to think about your breathing, and visualize your breath coming in through your nose, filling your lungs, and expanding your chest. Hold your breath for a few seconds and then release it. Once you have the rhythm of the breath, you can moderate it by counting in for eight counts and breathing out for eight counts. Start small if you need to, and only count for five breaths in and five out. There is no right or wrong way to do it. Do what you can, and with practice, like any new skill, you will improve. You can concentrate on this breathing technique for about five or ten minutes. It is okay if your mind begins to wander. Just let the thoughts come, and allow yourself to notice them. But do not be frustrated at having thoughts. Just observe you had a thought about this or that, and let it go without judgment. Then gently pull yourself back into the eight-count breathing technique. Once you practice this several times and have spent about five minutes breathing in and out, sit quietly in the silence. Feel the oxygen flow through your body, out to your fingertips, out through your toes. You can even visualize the oxygen going down to the earth beneath your feet, gathering energy and coming back up the body, up the spine to the top of the head, and beyond. Then just sit quietly for an additional five minutes, or until your body tells you it is time to come back.

Remember, all you need to do is a few minutes of measured breathing, a few minutes visualizing in silence and feeling the oxygen flowing through your body, and a few additional minutes of quiet time. If you just did this much, even in a sort of nap during the day, you would begin to see amazing results in your concentration and productivity. If you do not currently meditate and just finished trying this practice, you have completed your first meditation!

Guided meditation uses a CD or person to take you verbally through a meditative journey. You can be guided down a forest path that winds along a creek and past tall trees with thick bark and tangled roots. These suddenly give way to a thundering waterfall, pouring over a majestic cliff of smooth, water-worn rocks, where you sit and meditate, bringing you into deeper levels of consciousness. Actually, you can go anywhere in nature, watch a morning sunrise over the desert mountains, take a boat ride on a lake under a clear starry sky, hike through the majestic Rocky Mountains, or picture yourself in a small cabin surrounded by gentle rain falling on the rooftop. Alternatively, you can simply be guided through a relaxation technique within your own body that might begin at the top of your head, go through all the muscles in your body to the tips of your toes, and then breathe until you find yourself in deeper levels of consciousness. These types of meditations are usually guided in some way outside of yourself. It may even happen in a group, where the whole group is guided to have an experience that is similar yet very individual, since it all only happens within your own mind.

When my son was young and identified as hyperactive, I remember looking for something to help him slow down at the end of the day. He went to sleep every night with a guided relaxation and meditation tape. It was the same meditation tape every night. For a seven- or eight-year-old, it became symbolic, with slowing down his body and breathing, bringing his brain and energy to a place of quiet peace that subconsciously triggered it was time to sleep. The tape guided him through a relaxation piece first, which

115

became constant and comforting, along with a meditation piece that talked about self-esteem and strength of character. It was a lifesaver to help him go to sleep at night. And it was also a lifesaver for me as a young, single mother. Guided meditations are practical, useful, and plentiful to buy or find on the Internet. You just need to find one that you resonate with so that it helps you go into a deeper state of relaxation or consciousness with repeated practice.

There is something to be said for constantly using one piece of soft music that really helps you get into the meditative state. If it is not distracting and is low background music, it can enhance your practice as you learn what to expect each time you meditate. Consistent use of the same piece of music can help you get to a deep state of consciousness faster, because your body becomes used to the experience. The music can trigger the biological response to help you stay in meditation longer each time you practice. Your body begins to trust and relishes the process as it responds to a peaceful state of beingness that accompanies a meditation. Your body will begin to anticipate the deep sense of relaxation and help move you there more quickly. The mind will also tell you when the meditation is over. In a very interesting way you will just wake up. Your eyes will open, and you will know you have completed the meditation.

What begins to be really interesting is when you look at the clock and it is no longer a five-minute meditation. You realize thirty minutes have gone by, and you did not even know it. If you decide to take a quick five-minute rejuvenation at work, do not worry you will suddenly be gone for thirty minutes; your mind has an uncanny ability to exist in both places at once. You will begin to access that deeper consciousness for five minutes, while another part of your brain stays near the surface and lets you know it is time. It is amazing how it happens, but your mind just knows. You will not fall asleep, and you will not be gone too long. But you will feel vitally rested when you return!

Once you begin to find yourself in deeper states of meditation, the door begins to open to greater dimensions and levels of consciousness. Deeper meditation may even open the door to astral travel, or your spirit leaving the body. It is said that when the soul leaves the body, it stays connected through a cord of light from the body. Sometimes people may find they sort of fall asleep during this type of meditation, which happens if the conscious mind is not ready or prepared to view the soul's experience. The soul is always awake, but the conscious mind may not be ready to comprehend the actual experience itself. Trust the meditation anyway, even if you feel you do not stay awake. Your consciousness and spirit get exactly what they need out of each meditation. You will always be expanding your consciousness and growing, so trust the process.

Meditation brings one in tune with the universe in a sort of dreamy awakened state. To tap into your potential, you must tap into your inner world. You have an infinite amount of information within you, and meditation can help go within and discover if you take the time to center yourself and listen.

Metatron's Cube

The Merkaba, or Merkana as some call it, is the double pyramid within Metatron's Cube and often identified as the vehicle that carries the soul as we center ourselves in deep meditation. The whole essence of meditation at this level is focused on single-pointedness called the singularity. It is the Christ consciousness that is everywhere, the singularity of full awakening. Some may be familiar with the technological singularity we read about or watch in science fiction movies. Movies depict the technological singularity as being a time when artificial intelligence surpasses human intelligence. In meditation, it is the same single point of singularity, yet it isn't artificial intelligence that surpasses human intelligence; it is the Christ Consciousness, the intelligence of the universe that is greater. This singularity is the foundation of sacred geometry and the universal intelligence that is in all of us. This singularity is omnipotent unity, and it unfolds in duality here on earth and then returns to singularity in the Oneness of all. It is the source of all answers and the connection to the love within the entire universe. Connecting your soul to this singularity is achieved through advanced meditation and uses Metatron's Cube as the vehicle to carry the soul.

People who meditate will often begin their practice with a prayer of protection. When you are meditating and consciously place your soul within the Merkaba in deep meditation, it is useful to begin your meditation calling in the light of protection and surrounding yourself in a pillar of protective white light. Start by actually saying the words in your mind and calling on Archangel Michael to stand guard over the room. Consciously, in your mind's eye, place walls of protective light around the walls, ceiling, and floor of the room, so you are completely enclosed in the white light of protection while you meditate. This is sometimes comforting to people who do astral travel and believe their soul leaves the body for a while. As your soul of light travels among dimensional realms, you can ensure you are always enveloped in the white light of love and protection. You can also simply call down a pillar of white light to encompass your entire body or home at any time during the day. Picture the pillar of white light as a living life force of energy that will protect you at all times, and if you call it forth with intention, it will always be there. The white light of protection is a way of having the love of Source with you at any given time. The photons within your light body are intentionally activated through thought intention to align with the light of love, which brings a coherent energy to your meditation. You can do this before meditation, before going to bed at night, even before a difficult meeting at work. You can call on the protection of the white light at any time and trust that it will be there with you, protecting you for your highest good. Remember, belief is everything. All humans can create. Intentions, when stated with definite purpose and supported with firm belief, become our reality. Therefore, when you believe strongly that you are connected to the white light of protection or travel in your soul's Merkaba during meditations, you help to make it so.

As you begin a simple Merkaba meditation, it may also be important to mention hands. During meditation, hands are usually kept comfortable with palms up or open. But you can also keep your hands comfortable by cupping your hands in your lap, with the right hand underneath the left. Begin by sitting comfortably, position your hands, and then state a prayer of protection around the room. Next, center yourself in deep breathing for a few minutes, until you notice your mind is calm and your mind's eye is centered in the middle of your forehead. Use an Om tone if you are comfortable doing so. Then visualize your Merkaba in front of your body, slowly rotating as all things in the universe spin. Picture yourself moving into your Merkaba, slowly rotating, glowing with golden light, and holding your soul comfortably. Then allow yourself to be within a theta state for a period of time. You can do this in silence or with your chosen selection of soft, meditative music. Just ensure you are someplace quiet, without interruptions. When your soul is ready to return, you will suddenly emerge from your meditation feeling rested and relaxed. Write down any memories, experiences, or messages you remember for later review.

As you become more and more comfortable with meditation, you can begin to use this theta state to help you in your daily life. You can ask for clarity in your meditation or even put a thought intention into your consciousness to solve or resolve something in your life. It is helpful to jot down notes about images and thoughts that come through during the meditations, because they can hold clues and answers for you later. These are advanced techniques and skills that will help center and balance your life in amazing ways.

Emotions and Meditation

Breathing and meditation can also help manage emotions within the body. It is important to say a few words about emotion, because meditation can truly help balance emotions and impulsive emotional responses, as well as release emotional blocks that show up as energy blocks. A calm mind can help understand thoughts in subconscious programming that affect long-standing emotional issues in the body. Knowing that emotional imbalance can cause dis-ease in the body, which are mental blockages that may eventually become diseases, then mastering meditation to manage emotion can be a lifesaving, health-preserving technique.

Emotions and emotional blocks are very powerful things. Emotions define almost all our memories. All memories have some sort of emotional attachment to them. Did we feel really good about an experience or happy and want to experience it again? Or perhaps it was scary and fearful, so that it left us angry, sad, or broken in some way. In fact, we define our entire personal reality by how experiences make us feel. If our emotional body is blocked from past experiences of unresolved conflict or sorrow, our emotional body can affect our ability to move forward in balance and can squelch our ability to live our best centered life. Unresolved conflict can leave us feeling shame, unloved, or unworthy in some way. These unresolved issues and our inability to let them go can impact us throughout our entire lives. Unresolved issues can sabotage every relationship and every opportunity.

How can we move forward without resolving these issues, and how can we clear our emotional blocks? We tend to look for resolution outside ourselves, usually through manifesting a recurring event that keeps us spinning in the same cycles of emotional turmoil. Healing these emotional blocks through meditation is an individual process that begins with a personal awareness, along with an understanding of the repeating patterns in our lives. We can cultivate the ability to be the observer, to view our life and our reactions to our lives from an outside or more distanced perspective. We can achieve this even through meditation. We are the only ones who keep ourselves stuck in our programmed pattern of thinking that elicits a certain emotional response around the issues in our lives. Only our mind keeps us stuck in the whirlpool of our own life. Nothing keeps us there but our personal thinking patterns. It can take a lifetime to break out of the patterns, or perhaps many lifetimes. What a shame to give away so much of our precious lives!

Negative emotions pull us down, control our actions, and paralyze our ability to be in control. We are 100 percent responsible for what happens to us. Even if something happens that is very damaging and dark, out of our control, we have the opportunity to decide now to let it define us or our happiness ... or not. Unhappiness is a dense place for consciousness to live. It is buying into a lower reality grid that mingles with other unhappy souls. It is the matrix cocreated with other individuals stuck in the way they are choosing to see their lives. The way we view life is everything; the key is to change our view. Meditate daily to bring yourself into the frequency of love, and send out your coherent energy to heal others with similar negative or unhappy thinking patterns. As you focus energy on helping to heal others, you heal yourself. Miraculously, you may begin to view your own situation differently. Ask Source to help with the release of the mental thinking, anger, or sadness that keeps you stuck in the issue, and ask for circumstances, experiences, and events that will serve the highest good for all involved.

We need our emotions to experience life, which in turn provide experiences that connect us to our spiritual self as we grow and learn. Learning to let go and forgive, whatever the circumstances, might be the most important thing we learn to do. Of everything presented in this book, the most important thing to remember may be that living a centered life may begin with this one simple task: forgive and let go. Letting go is easier said than done, but it can happen, and it can happen through meditation. Using deeper levels of consciousness and attaining higher levels of the love frequency makes negative events seem much less relevant and puts them in perspective. Living within the universal flow and remembering that we are all One help us see that for whatever reason a particular experience came into our life, it happened at a soul level with something in the experience for us to learn. Through greater awareness of our universal connectedness, we begin to realize each person involved in our specific situation had his or her own lesson to learn. The reality was cocreated in order for each to experience their respective lessons. Our choice now is to learn and let it go. However, because we each can exercise free will, you can also choose to hang on and create other recurring experiences that will replicate the same lessons in this lifetime or another, over and over again.

There is a natural or logical connection between our divine light and our inner heart. Our light is coherent and transmitted from within. Our heart is the place where our personal truths come together and from which we send forth our own divine light. Our divine light is a frequency just as all energy is a frequency. This frequency is shaped, harmonized, and fed by our thoughts, actions, love, and core beliefs. It is important to monitor what frequencies we choose to store in our inner heart. What do you hold in your heart? Be reflective, be aware, meditate, love, forgive, and let go!

Food for Thought

Try working on breathing techniques every day. Learn to breathe deeply, because oxygen feeds the body and mind. It will activate the energy centers as you visualize your breath moving through the body up and down the spine. Visualize the breath anchoring you to the earth to help ground you as go about your day or during a specific meditation process.

Try various meditation techniques. Find a guided meditation selection to help you with both relaxation and meditation. Try to select a specific piece of music to be played each time you sit and meditate formally. The music can help bring you into a meditative state more quickly with practice.

Try practicing meditation daily, taking one step at a time. Meditation is an excellent way to begin to develop a focused mind. Most people are shocked when they begin meditating to find out how undisciplined their mind is and how often thoughts float in, whether or not they are wanted. Both practice and the power of concentration will help build self-discipline and the willpower to connect within. Do not give up.

Write down thoughts, impressions, visions, or "dreams" you may have during your meditations. They can be insightful when you read them later, especially if you discover a recurring theme.

Advanced meditators can even practice more than once a day. Become clear in advance about what you want out of the meditation. Is it just to relax and rejuvenate, or is there something you need help resolving? Advanced meditators might also consider calling in the white light for protection. This is a way of protecting your meditation space by visualizing white, healing love energy coming down in a column and surrounding you, your room, and your home. This visualization centers you and sets up the mental image that you are ready to go within yourself in quiet meditation. Begin deep breathing, which oxygenates the body, for five minutes before drifting into the meditation itself. When all aspects of consciousness are connected, we can gain insight into our overall purpose in life.

Try working toward developing more self-discipline. It is important to note there is a difference between concentration and self-discipline. Concentration is holding your mind on something you choose. Self-discipline is holding your mind in a certain direction for a long time. Both require development and determination. There is an art to training and practicing toward developing a mind that can concentrate and learn to be self-disciplined. Most people start new things, like meditating, but do not follow through long enough for it to become a habit. It has been said that doing something for twenty-one days will begin to make it a habit that results in a greater ability to follow through.

Try focusing on any emotional memories that are not serving your higher good, so you can bring them forward and present. Be aware of the emotional memory and the observer of your life within your meditation. Try to identify the lesson for you to understand and your role in the experience or event. Was there something that you might need to learn from the overall experience? Send the experience coherent love energy for all involved to help resolve hurtful feelings. Learn to let the emotional experience go, along with any attachments or thinking habits you may have about the issue.

Consider advanced forms of meditation. Barbara Marciniak, in *Bringers of the Dawn*, talks about spinning as a technique for greater clarity. Begin with deep breathing while in a standing position. Place your arms and hands straight out in front of you, chest level, with palms together. Keeping your hands as the center point, turn in a circle. Spin your body counterclockwise, in a circle moving to your right. This aids in spinning the chakra systems and allows you greater access to interpret data and information you may receive in this state. It does not need to be rapid spinning, but if you practice and build up to spinning thirty-three times, which is a sacred number, at least once a day you will achieve even greater levels of consciousness. Always write down your experiences afterward.

Finally, drink a lot of water when you meditate. Water is a great purifier and conductor. Always put a thought intention into your water to purify it. Send it light, and intentionally ask for enhanced meditative experiences through blessing and drinking the water.

CHAPTER 8

Chakras and Energy Connections

> There is deep wisdom within our very flesh, if
> we can only come to our senses and feel it.
> —Elizabeth A. Behnke

T he wisdom of chakra energy has been used by Eastern and
Western practitioners for many years. The chakras are included
here to draw a deeper connection between the energy that surrounds
our individual bodies within our own EMF and to understand how
that energy interacts with us physically, mentally, and spiritually.
In the Eastern tradition, chakras are centers of Prana, life force,
or vital energy that flow through the body. The word *chakra* comes
from the Sanskrit word meaning wheel or turning. Everything
in the universe turns, from the orbiting of the solar system, to the
planets, to the atoms in our bodies, and even the Torus energy field
around all things. It is the way of the cosmos to spin or rotate, and
the energy in the chakra system spins in the same way.

The earliest written account of the chakras is believed to be
part of the Vedas, an old group of texts written in traditional Vedic
Sanskrit in ancient India and said to have originated between 1500
and 1000 BCE. The Vedas are the basic writings of the Hindu faith
but also have an influence on Buddhism. Interestingly, they were
also part of the ancient knowledge held in the library of Alexandria
in Egypt. An expansion beyond the types of material contained
in the oldest Veda, the Rig Veda, is found in the Atharva Veda,
another of the four Vedic Books. The Atharva Veda holds numerous

texts in which meditation is discussed in addition to incantations and other material found in the Rig Veda. It is believed that the Artharva Veda was written around 200 BCE but may have been comprised much earlier, about 1000 BCE.

Ancient writing in India expanded beyond the Vedas with discussions that focused on the importance of meditation as a method to unite the soul with ultimate truth. This material is found in a body of writing called the Upanishads, which were a continuation of the Vedic philosophy and written more recently than the Vedas, between 800 and 400 BCE. The Upanishads are also important for introducing the well-known concept of karma, the cumulative effects of a person's actions. India's ancient texts also contain the narrative history of the universe from creation to destruction, including the lineage of kings and Hindu cosmology. Material of this type is found in the Puranas, which are post-Vedic texts. Yogic practice is explained in later texts called the Yoga Sutras. The practice of yoga is used to energize the chakra systems in the body through poses and breathing techniques. However, the ultimate energy source within the body is said to be the Kundalini energy, which is considered to be the Mother of the Universe. Kundalini energy is presented and described in the Puranas as well. Kundalini energy is both powerful and important and is worth investigating in a bit more detail.

The Kundalini is described as one of the esoteric components of the inner body or energy channels. It is said to be a coiled source of residual power of pure desire. The energy is referred to as a coiled serpent and lies dormant until a true seeker activates this powerful energy source through meditation and advanced yogic practice. Practitioners describe it as a source of orgasmic electricity, shooting up the chakra centers on two nerve currents aligned in the spinal column. It is also said that the Kundalini experience is the one and only way of attaining divine wisdom or awakening of inner knowledge that brings pure joy and pure love. Many people have active Kundalini energy in the body, especially in the pelvic region, where it lies coiled at the base of the spine. Meditation, yoga, stretching, and exercise can all begin to activate this powerful energy. The key is to recognize it in the body and direct it through the chakra areas and up the spine. The alignment and health of the chakra energies should be mastered before one can truly direct this powerful experience.

Chakras have been primarily referred to as seven major spinning energy centers or vortexes within the body that generate vibration and light. Some believe opening the chakra centers heightens the consciousness of the individual. The term "consciousness" refers to an individual's state of mind, and, therefore, the chakras are tied to mental development that helps one attain enlightenment through cleansing and meditation. The chakras are not physical; they are aspects of consciousness and frequency or vibration. It should be noted here that in many circles, it is believed the energies around the body have evolved to a place where the original seven chakra centers are expanding in number and changing their color dynamics. There is a new chakra system that includes a total of thirteen chakra energy points on the body. This includes the original seven, which will be discussed below, as well as a well-of-dreams chakra at the back base of the skull and a pituitary chakra at the front. There is also the addition of a masculine and feminine chakra, located just above the physical body on each person. There are actually even more chakras that work on the etheric realm, acting almost like an antenna above and below the body. Those will be discussed more later. The original seven and two others are included in the following chakra descriptions.

The Chopra Center, started by the famous endocrinologist and metaphysician Deepak Chopra, talks about the seven chakra energy centers serving as junction points between the body and consciousness or between matter and the mind, according to Tantric tradition. The spinning vortexes receive the vital life force energy that feeds the body, mind, and soul and connect an individual to the outside world and everyone he or she comes in contact with each day.

Aligned with bodily functions, these seven centers are arranged vertically up the spine, from the base of the spine to the top of the head, and they regulate the flow of energy throughout the body. They interact with the body through two major body systems: the endocrine, the body's main control mechanism, and the nervous systems. The original seven chakras are tied to specific parts of the biological body, and it is vital and necessary to clean and nurture them for centered living. Each chakra is associated with or has governance over the parts of the body associated with the respective endocrine gland and related group of nerves. The endocrine system produces hormones, or chemical messengers, that secrete into the bloodstream and induce physical processes. These processes are responsible for adjusting hormone levels to keep the body in optimum health. This link between energy and the biological systems in the body represents the holistic nature of needing to maintain balance in the emotional, physical, and mental parts of self. The balance of the biological systems and our physical and etheric selves is intrinsically connected.

Through aging, illness, environmental toxins, and absorption of negativity in our lives, the chakras begin to break down, darken, and slow their rate of spinning. It is believed that the ancients knew this and designed mantras and meditation techniques to maintain the vitality and vibrational rate of the chakras. Activation and balance of the energy flowing through the chakras allows the mind to connect with the higher or spiritual self; everything is aligned in unity. The original seven main chakras are important for energy work and developing greater health, vitality, and spiritual enlightenment. Two additional chakras will be discussed, one for grounding of the body and the other for opening the crown chakra. Both are important extensions of the current seven major energy systems. These are all explained in relation to function, color, and meaning for health and contemplation. It is never too late to begin linking to the energy around your body and intentionally thinking healing thoughts for your internal systems to provide optimal health. No doubt the majority of humans interacting with the environment daily would need intentional meditation to regularly enhance and clean these energy systems.

The first energy center mentioned here is not part of the original seven listed in most books, but it is important to begin with the earth star or earth chakra. Its purpose is to ground the body to the healing energy of the earth. It is associated with the colors black or brown and is located twelve to eighteen inches below the soles of the feet. The earth chakra connects with the magnetic core of the earth and helps ground the body. The purpose of grounding is to draw the energies of the earth to you, secure you to the physical world, protect you as you go about your daily activities, and release excess energies in your body. Many things interfere and tend to unground you during the day including the environmental disruptors mentioned earlier. Physically walking or sitting on the earth is another way to connect to this powerful grounding chakra.

The base or root chakra is the first of the seven major chakras and is located at the base of the spine. This chakra is associated with the color red and the feeling of being centered. It is part of your core, your pelvic area, which is the centering part of your body. It is strongly associated with and focused on the physical aspects of life, as well as the area of the body where your ambitions, interests, and sex drive originate. The root chakra influences the ability to feel sexually comfortable, and it is tied to circulation, support, survival, base instincts, and protection. It is also associated with male reproductive glands and the kidneys, which produce adrenaline connecting to the fight-or-flight response. The root chakra is the center for overall physical energy, which is why it is so important to exercise and build a strong body core.

The navel or sacral chakra is located just below the navel and corresponds to the color orange. This is the chakra for relationships, emotions, sensuality, intimacy, and sexuality. The feminine nature of this chakra emerges through governing the female reproductive organs, genitals, bladder, and lower back. It deals with the concepts of feeling, clairsentience, commitment, security, and emotions. The sacral chakra ensures your emotional life operates in a healthy way. The hormonal system governed by this chakra includes the ovaries and controls the level of estrogen and progesterone in the body. Regular balancing of this chakra is critical for emotional intimacy, passion, and sexuality.

It is important to note that humans have both masculine and feminine energy centers within the body because of the influence of the first two main chakras. The masculine and feminine energy has nothing to do with gender. Both masculine and feminine energy representations are changing and becoming balanced on earth today. They are often referred to as divine masculine and divine feminine, but again, they are not gender specific. Think of masculine energy as the dominant energy on the earth for thousands of years. It was action-oriented, commanding, and authoritative energy. Feminine energy has been on earth as well but is emerging as a stronger presence in the world. It is defined as compassionate, understanding, and nurturing, an expansion of higher spirituality in all people. Both forms of energy are necessary for human creation and expression, and exist within everyone.

The stomach or solar plexus chakra, located right below the breastbone and between the base of the sternum and the navel, is the third main chakra and corresponds to the color yellow. The solar plexus chakra focuses on responsibility for others, caring for others, self-confidence, self-esteem, the ego, personal power, self-worth, clarity, and creativity. It governs the effective flow of energy throughout the body. Improving the energy in this area may clear problems that have to do with lack or limitations. This is the chakra responsible for manifestation on all levels, including talents, abilities, spirituality, money, good health, and relationships. It influences the physical areas of the stomach, upper intestines, upper back, and upper spine. It governs the pancreas, which secretes substances for the digestion of food. This includes insulin, which influences blood sugar. Balancing the solar plexus chakra is critical for sufficient self-esteem.

It is important to notice how these first three chakras influence many core aspects of life. The physical properties associated with this stomach to pelvic region holds emotional, sexual, and basic instinctual aspects of daily life. A regular exercise routine that strengthens the core, like Pilates or yoga, along with healthy food make all the difference in your energy and daily outlook. In fact, exercise, water, and healthy food can do much to balance these key energy centers and eliminate energy blockages, too. Many people begin to activate the Kundalini, which affects a sort of spiritual sexuality in the body. As you begin to practice with the Kundalini energy, you can first feel it moving through this region of the body. Continued work can help move this powerful energy from the sexual center of the body to the heart portal and beyond.

The heart chakra is associated with the color green. This chakra is located in the center of the chest and vibrates with an energy that assists one to live life from the heart, where love, compassion, and happiness are generated. It is the fourth and central chakra of the seven. Strengthening peace and unconditional love, this chakra manifests the meaning of loving in a sacred sense and is one of the higher vibrational chakras. The heart chakra is associated with the circulatory system and thymus gland. The thymus produces lymphocytes, which form a vital part of the body's immune response. The energy from this chakra holds healing elements and is critical for group consciousness and spirituality.

If the first three chakras hold the foundation of the body for living physically here on earth, the heart chakra is the center point of healing energy, loving energy, and spiritual energy entering and leaving the body. It holds a higher vibration and can be directed through intentional thought, as we have seen through HeartMath's research. The heart chakra rotates as all chakras rotate, but within that energy, there is a spiritual vibration. When healthy and clear, this vibration helps connect to Source. Clearing this chakra not only involves color and energy alignment but also emotional clearing and opening the vortex, or heart portal, to the influx and outflow of the divine love energy. The health of the first three chakras links to the immune response of the heart, and deep breathing, practice, and sending love energy through intention and meditation link these systems spiritually. Working with the Kundalini energy as it moves up the spine to the heart portal can open the energy pathways of the heart to sending and receiving a deeper and more profound love from the heart.

The throat chakra is associated with communication and the color blue; it is your personal voice. This fifth chakra is located in the neck, above the collarbone. It assists in the truthful and honest expression of ideas. The throat chakra also governs hearing, speaking, listening, and communicating, which are all forms of self-expression. The energy of the chakra manages the health of the physical throat but also etheric communication, hearing your inner voice, and your psychic abilities. The health of the throat chakra is critical for communication, speech, writing and thought expression.

The throat chakra is also associated with the respiratory system and thyroid gland. The thyroid produces the hormone thyroxin, which controls the rate at which the body converts food into useful energy.

The third eye chakra is associated with the colors purple or indigo and is located behind the forehead, above the eyebrows. It is thought to be in the site of the pineal gland, where our visionary abilities emerge. A clear third eye chakra can help develop psychic abilities, such as clairvoyance or the ability to see things psychically; clairaudience, the ability to hear things psychically; and clairsentience, the ability to feel things psychically. It also aids in strengthening your intuition. The third eye chakra holds the concept of seeing in a spiritual sense, often associated with seeing within the pineal gland. When the pineal begins to open, people often feel a tingling in this area. The third eye chakra is associated with the autonomic nervous system and the pituitary gland as well. The pituitary gland releases hormones influencing the entire body chemistry. Good health of this chakra is critical for good intuition and psychic powers.

We now see how the energy and collective chakra vibration has moved into a more cerebral aspect, since both the throat and third eye chakras govern elements of the unseen. Communication is basically thought, and we have seen how thought, our own thoughts, affect our lives. The third eye is intuition or energy that exists in consciousness, or perhaps the theta state. Good chakra clearing or meditation always moves from the base, the core, first, through the center vortex of the love energy, and up to the collective consciousness. When you practice deep breathing for chakra balancing, you breathe up the spine, but you also come back down. In fact, an advanced breathing technique brings the breath up the front of the body, through the heart, and out the back, up the back and around the head, down the front of the head and through the heart once again, and down the back of the body around the pelvis. The breath is forming the infinity shape through the chakras, crossing through the center vortex—the heart.

The crown chakra is associated with the color violet and is the last of the major chakras. This chakra is located just above the top of the head. This is the point where spirit introduces energy from the higher realms to be distributed throughout the body. It is the chakra that governs the "knowing" in a spiritual sense, the gift of psychic knowing ethereally. Crown chakra energy relates to spirituality, selflessness, empathy, and humanitarianism. It is where one connects with the higher self, intelligence in spirit, higher consciousness, and deep thought. The crown chakra is associated with the central nervous system and the pineal gland. It is also the center of enlightenment, dynamic thought, truth, oneness, and our ability to gain wisdom and be one with the world. Enlightenment and expansive thinking depend greatly on this crucial chakra.

All seven major chakras are independent but also part of the greater energy system. In fact, they are very dependent on each other to be healthy and vibrant. It starts with the energy of the base chakra, which is tied to physical living day to day and moves up the spine to connect your physical self with the collective consciousness. We mentioned previously that scientists, in monitoring the flow of biophotons in the body, found these light particles in every cell and in our DNA. We also know some believe the nervous system is a sort of fiber-optic highway that carries biophotons throughout the body. We know that the light holds actual information that can be carried throughout the body as well. And we just learned the crown chakra is associated with the central nervous system and pineal gland. It is where positive energy enters the body to be distributed throughout the body. These original major chakra centers are all important to living spiritually and within the life flow.

The final chakra shared here is found above the crown chakra. The soul star chakra, sometimes called the seat of the soul, is associated with the color white and governs the stellar gateway between it and the crown chakra. Divine light and energy filter down using the stellar gateway and into the crown chakra for distribution throughout the body. This expansive, infinite light energy aligns spiritually to our heart, infusing divine wisdom and spiritual compassion. It is associated with the origin of enlightenment and ascension, often believed to be Christ Consciousness. Achieving this uses a process of internally letting go and allowing the light of the divine Spirit to guide the way ethereally.

Healing the Chakras

Chakras can influence all consciousness experienced within and without the body. When you feel tension and stress, the thought patterns in your brain are affected, and the stress is translated into the biological functions in the body. Stress and tension will also manifest in blockages within the chakra system. Over a period of time, such a blockage can manifest into a physical disease.

Chakra energies interact with the physical body through an intricate system of nerve endings that communicate back and forth through the biophotons of light. One biophoton can carry about four megabytes of information, including an individual's complete DNA makeup as well as memories and soul experiences. New biophoton research shows the astounding intensity with which biophotons communicate at the cellular level within the body. It is believed that very refined tuning occurs in the molecular processes that emit the biophotons. The biophotons transfer this energy to the cell surface, so genetic receptors receive the information at an even wider level of vibrational frequency. The spinning energy of the chakras, in essence, speaks to the body in the language of energy and light.

The *Review*, a Massachusetts Institute of Technology magazine for innovation, states that a growing body of evidence suggests the molecular machinery of life emits and absorbs photons. Evidence shows this light is a new form of cellular communication. In May of 2012 the *Review* stated "Bio photon streams consist of short quasi periodic bursts, which are remarkably similar to those used to send binary data over a noisy channel". They were able to isolate opportunities for communication to happen, similar to binary code, within routine bodily functions. Even though we do not yet understand the communication, we know it is happening.

To date, little research has actually been done on chakras. However, Dr. Hiroshi Motoyama bridges the worlds of both science and spirituality. He holds two doctorate degrees and is also a Shinto priest. Several significant experiments regarding chakras have been conducted under his auspices. He successfully developed a chakra instrument that detects minute electrical magnetic and optical changes that occur in the immediate environment. In 1992 he created the California Institute in Human Science, whose cutting edge 2012 conference centered on the research of consciousness and healing. His research reflects the revolutionary influence subtle energy has on practice, science, and the healing arts, including the chakra system.

Healing unbalanced chakras can come in many forms. Sound, light, and meditative practices are all used to balance and heal the chakra systems. Sound healing of the chakras is as old as Atlantis but only recently seems to be regaining recognition. Sound healing is the educated use of techniques and technologies that use the energies and vibrations of sound to expand consciousness and heal the systems of the body. It is based on the science that all things vibrate at various frequencies and that sound and vibration can impact matter in specific ways. The study of cymatics shows sound creates geometric patterns in matter. Cymatics is the study of visible sound in vibration, visible through some sort of medium but measured in the resulting patterning based on the frequency of the vibratory sound. Cymatics is the process of visually seeing the inherent geometric shapes within sound and music. Sound can also alter brain waves to help people with sleep disorders and facilitate creative expression. Research shows improvement in sound treatments for children with learning disabilities and other disorders. Doctors have shown early results using the resonant sound frequency of specific healthy organs in the body to heal diseased organs of the same type.

Sound healing can be generated naturally from toning, chanting, shamanic drumming, and tones from crystals bowls and tuning forks, as well as computerized or soundboard-generated music. Healers use specific techniques for chakra treatment that include a combination of tuning forks, crystal bowls, Tibetan bowls, voice, and computerized soundtracks to align chakras and balance the energies. Results have shown sound healing works at the 528-hertz frequency. Some believe the entire natural world—from the blades of grass to the vibrations received from the sun—vibrates at the level of 528 hertz. They believe it is the universal vibration that can bring humans back into healthy resonance. This concept is explored further in chapter 10 on healing.

Light healing has also gained recognition as a way to rebalance ailing chakras. It consists of infusing the body with a variety of light combinations to balance chakras, relieve chronic pain, and treat emotional stress, grief, or depression. Some claim it helps children with attention deficit disorder or attention deficit hyperactivity disorder.

Light healing works through light refraction. As white light enters a prism, the speed at which it travels changes, causing the light to be refracted in a new angle. The degree of the bending of the light's path depends on the angle of the beam sending the light. The colors are dispersed in the colors of a prism, which are, interestingly, the colors that match the seven major chakras. Light therapists use the refracted light as it enters the body to assist in the balancing process. New technologies are still emerging, and new research uses a more advanced light emitting diode (LED) system to provide light healing sessions at some alternative clinics.

Knowing the body is 80 percent water and that all cells house biophotons, it is not surprising that our bodies may be affected in some way and possibly healed through light and sound. The work now is to find the correct frequency and group of sounds or vibrations that can bring a healing resonance throughout the body.

Chakras are the interface point between physical and nonphysical form. In addition to the seven chakra centers located in the body, there are over seventy-two chakras on the ethereal body, of which twenty-two work with our inner self. All seventy-two chakras are aligned above the head and specifically designed to act as kind of a tuning antenna. They are aligned with sound, like a note on a scale. It is believed they intercept specific wavelengths of energy containing light information in the energy fields around the body and bring that information down into the body structure itself, even to the cellular level. Meditative practice can help tap into these vibrant energy centers. Understanding how the energy fields move around and through the body and how they function together with the body's biological systems can make the difference when choosing healing practices that align the chakras for optimal living.

As you learn to come from a place of love and intention every day, you can begin to consider your bonded relationship to another. It is important to say a few words about attraction, relationships, and sexuality, as this is also a vast component of life on earth and energy connections. A clear chakra aura and emotional field can open you up to having genuine rather than incomplete relationships. Like attracts like, and what we send out will be met with a response from someone. Have you ever wondered why you may be attracted to one person and not another? Perhaps there is an initial attraction of some kind that goes away fairly quickly. Our initial attraction often tends to be of a sexual nature. One person tends to activate your sexual center energetically, while someone else may not. You are often attracted to someone who carries a similar energy field or patterning, and more than one person can match. You have a circuitry within you that is activated on different levels by different people. Think of the chakras; the first three chakras are within your pelvic region. Someone may match your energy in a physical attraction, your sexual center, where a sexual compatibility exists. Or on another level, you may love someone dearly, because you match circuitry through the heart center but not necessarily through the sexual center. Or you may connect with someone mentally in a shared sense of intelligence and sense of humor, but never really love the person intimately or be physically attracted to him or her.

Each of these energy points functions independently, like a radar going out in the world, or they can function jointly to find a true match. A true relationship exists between two people when they are connected with matched circuitry in each of these energy points. When you find someone you connect with, you may open each other's heart and complete the circuitry. His or her presence makes you want to become a better person and vice versa, so together you make a whole. You may find several individuals who connect in different ways, or you may find someone who connects with your soul circuitry. But it is rare to find one who fits them all. Some people's frequencies are more complementary than others. Together, your fields complement one another. This connected circuitry is a communication mechanism that is "felt" between people who have strong compatible fields.

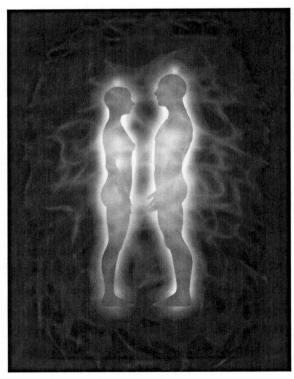

Connected Energy

Like the chakras, the kundalini energy force in the body can also come into play in very powerful ways between two people who have matched circuitry. Think of two people who come together in passion, a lust that is hard to control and deny. Chances are the sexual circuitry is so complete it has activated the kundalini within the sexual center, beginning to move it up the spine. This can happen without the two individuals actually being aware of these energy changes or kundalini activations. They simply know their sexual passion is sweet and strong. If two people come together in this way but do not match any other circuitry, the passion can often be destructive and unhealthy. However, if two people find this passion and open their heart centers to love, it can provide the basis for a true relationship to grow. When two people are open to this sacred expression through understanding, they can harness the sexual passion while channeling the kundalini energy up to the heart center and ultimately through the crown chakra as the most powerful form of the sexual experience, love experience, and spiritual experience united as one.

In *Bringers of the Dawn*, author Barbara Marciniak talks about sexuality as raising frequency levels in the body. Every sexual experience exchanges frequencies; even hugging someone exchanges frequencies between two people. She says a sexual experience gives off a hormonal release inside the body, which opens the energy of the cells and transfers one person's essence to another. This is why you may feel you cannot get someone's sex or energy off of you. If you have had a sexual experience with someone and have exchanged frequencies, but you no longer want to be together, you may have a hard time with the electromagnetic exchange that has been experienced by you both. She says that expressing oneself sexually should encourage our greatest growth energetically and should be shared. Yet people often share sexual experiences without thinking about the greater role sexuality provides.

When one is on the path of soul growth, it is also natural for someone to experience a period of sexual dormancy. It is more important to hold sacred who you are in the world and then exchange a sexual frequency with someone you choose. If you are bonding yourself and chemically exchanging with someone you do not want to be with, you take on their "stuff," too. Marciniak states that the truth of sexuality is not only procreation or pleasure but that sex can also open frequencies that align with spiritual growth, like kundalini activation between people. Sexual experience can be used as a method of evolving spiritually, emotionally, and cosmically if you have a partner who is of your shared circuitry and willing to share the spiritual growth.

Achieving this level of relationship requires trust, understanding, and a desire for shared spiritual growth. Our sexuality is affected by all our past programming and negative thinking patterns, and these patterns around sexuality are subject to the personal emotional work we must do to prepare for a greater intimate relationship and sexual connection. That is why it is so important that each person is sovereign in his or her individual path of enlightenment. Then two people, each whole within themselves, can choose to be bonded together in this way. The sexual experience between the two can then be more tantric in nature. Tantric sex—or tantra, the phrase for sacred sexuality—has been written about in ancient yogic texts and more modern books, like the *Kama Sutra*. The goal is not to achieve an orgasm but to channel all the sexual energy that would normally leave during orgasm back into the body, moving it up your energy centers, and increasing potent sexual, kundalini energy, and intimacy with your partner. It is through this higher form of energy, and then orgasm, that frequencies are opened and shared. Sacred sexual experiences are capable of elevating each person to a higher spiritual plane. Choosing a sexual partner can be much more than finding simple pleasure. When shared with someone you love and trust, you can grow together to experience higher forms of intimacy and spirituality through sexual expression.

Food for Thought

Try taking time to learn about the chakras and really understand the connection between the energy and biological functions of each chakra point in the body.

Try visualizing each chakra during your daily meditation. When you get comfortable with your meditation practice, move through each of the chakras, visualizing the chakra colors and the spinning energy at the beginning of a meditation. This will help keep the chakras active. You can include a thought intention of clearing and healing them, too.

Use alternative meditations to clear the chakras. For many people, meditation is the generally accepted method for using your own healing abilities with thought intention to bring the chakras in balance in the etheric field. Chakra meditations with music are plentiful on the Internet and are an excellent source for moving you through the meditative process to heal each individual chakra. A chakra activation meditation practice is recommended weekly, unless you live in an area full of environmental disruptors; then three or more times a week is useful.

Try setting up a daily exercise program. Practicing a simple routine such as yoga, stretching, or brisk walking will begin to move energy in the body and assist in breaking up blocked energy patches. It will also enhance your breathing techniques.

Again, drink a lot of water. Because water is a wonderful purifier and conductor, first purify it with your intention. Send light to the water intentionally to enhance meditative experiences through blessing and drinking the water. You will see the importance and usefulness of pure water as a recurring theme in each of the remaining chapters.

CHAPTER 9

The Pineal Gland and Inner Health

The key to growth is the introduction of higher
dimensions of consciousness into our awareness.
—Lao Tzu

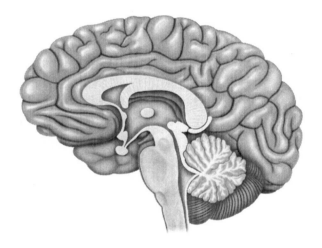

The Pineal Gland

Ancient teachings and current science are beginning to align and tell us a great deal about consciousness, our thoughts, and how they can direct, manifest, and heal our lives in profound ways. To provide a holistic view of our mind's capabilities to connect with the conscious realm within and without, we must consider another phenomenon that links back to ancient knowledge. The connections lie in the symbolism tied to every ancient culture and

142

religious origin, including the Vatican. The mystery surrounds the pineal gland, a small, pinecone-shaped gland located in the precise geometric center of the brain. It is often referred to as the mystery gland or third eye. Metaphysically speaking, it is the place responsible for psychic visions and possibly even soul travel. This tiny gland, what we know about it medically and scientifically, and what we believe about it metaphysically, is that it is an amazing source of incredible intrigue. Like the kundalini energy in the body, the pineal gland is a source of great power and should be viewed with reverence and respect. Its health and well-being is of utmost importance, yet it is currently damaged and crippled in most people.

Biologically, the pineal gland is part of the endocrine system and produces several important hormones, including melatonin. Melatonin is a derivative of serotonin and specifically connects the endocrine system with the nervous system. The pineal converts signals from nerve endings into hormone signals that induce hormonal release. The pineal has five main functions.

- Secretes melatonin
- Regulates the endocrine functions
- Converts nervous system signals to endocrine signals
- Causes feelings of sleepiness
- Influences sexual development

The pineal is activated by the light and dark differences of day and night and controls various biorhythms in the body. It also directs the body's thirst, hunger, and sexual desire. Ultimately, it is the biological clock that determines our aging process.

Pineal glands are rich, healthy, and larger in children. But as we age, it reduces to the size of a pea as it undergoes a detrimental, gradual calcification process. The optimum size of the healthy pineal gland, when fully engorged and activated, is that of a grape. By the time we become teenagers, it is heavily calcified. Researchers believe this is a direct result of negative dietary and environmental factors.

Calcification is the buildup of calcium phosphate crystals in various parts of the body. It is caused by nano bacteria, tiny microorganisms that form calcium phosphate shields around themselves to protect them from our immune system. New research is also finding this development of protective shields may be the same process that protects cells in the body that cause most diseases, from arthritis to stroke and even cancer. It has only been in the last fifty or sixty years that our diets and food systems have become so detrimental to our bodies. Some might argue that sixty years ago diets might have been deficient in many other vitamins. And while this is true, the advent of processed foods, preservatives, water additives, food additives, and pesticides are wreaking havoc on us biologically today.

The calcification of the pineal gland is due to the harmful effects of substances found in our environment. These include mercury, which is found in fish and dental fillings; fluoride chemicals found in our public water systems and in our toothpaste; hormones and additives put into processed foods; sugars and artificial sweeteners; pesticides; alcohol; and smoking. Cell phones are also pinpointed as potentially harmful because cell phones emit radiofrequency energy, a form of non-ionizing electromagnetic radiation, which can be absorbed by tissues closest to where the phone is held.

> The only known biological effect of radiofrequency energy is heating. The ability of microwave ovens to heat food is one example of this effect of radiofrequency energy. Radiofrequency exposure from cell phone use does cause heating; however, it is not sufficient to measurably increase body temperature.

> A recent study showed that when people used a cell phone for 50 minutes, brain tissues on the same side of the head as the phone's antenna metabolized more glucose than did tissues on the opposite side of the brain. The researchers noted that the results are preliminary,

and possible health outcomes from this increase in glucose metabolism are still unknown (National Cancer Institute).

Anyone who talks on the phone for long periods of time knows the extent to which their phone heats and feels against their heads, and the proximity of this radiofrequency energy to all brain functions in addition to the pineal.

The biggest culprit to pineal calcification seems to be sodium fluoride, the white chemical found in drinking water and almost all types of toothpaste in the United States. The chemical surprisingly is also found in rat poison. Even medications from pharmacologists include sodium fluoride.

A study in *Scientific American* concluded that "fluoride can subtly alter endocrine function, especially in the thyroid, the gland that produces hormones regulating growth and metabolism." This study also noted fluoride poisoning was linked to many other ailments in addition to pineal gland calcification. There are at least thirty-six other studies linking sodium fluoride with reduced IQ in children as well.

The study in *Scientific American* also mentions that over twelve hundred professionals have urged Congress to cease water fluoridation, because scientific evidence indicated fluoridation is ineffective and produces serious health risks. Fluoride is present in some level in water everywhere, yet it is still added to more than 60 percent of all public water systems in the United States and to some bottled water purchased from stores. More people in the United States drink fluoridated water than in the rest of the world combined.

Toothpaste is another source of sodium fluoride entering the system. Though touted as minimizing the formation of cavities in the teeth, the Food and Drug Administration in 1997 ordered toothpaste manufacturers to add a poison warning to all fluoride toothpastes sold in the United States. While fatalities from sodium fluoride ingestion are rare, acute fluoride poisoning is not. The report says fluoride in foods, beverages, medicines, and dental products can result in fluoride overconsumption. Fluoride overconsumption is really only visible in young children manifested as dental fluorosis (white spotted, yellow, brown, or pitted teeth). We normally cannot see the effects of fluoride overconsumption in the rest of the body as we get older which adds to the health risks.

Reviewing the label on most packaged foods can seem like reading a science book when you look at the list of preservatives contained in the food. As a rule of thumb, reading the ingredients on packages can help, and if you cannot pronounce it, you probably should not eat it. Years ago, nutritionists began to talk about only shopping for food around the outside edges of the grocery store. This is where the whole or natural foods are generally found. In addition, sodium fluoride and pesticides are found in soda, red meat, and on inorganic fruits and vegetables. These are all types of foods that fill our daily intake of nutrition.

One of the highest sources of natural sodium fluoride in a food is green tea. Green tea is often touted as better for you because of its high antioxidant content. Yet green tea has been found to contain higher levels of natural sodium fluoride than most other foods. Green tea is not bad for you if it was the only source of sodium fluoride; it is the slow poisoning in the cumulative effects from many sources that is the problem.

The flood of sodium fluoride in water and food creates other, more serious health problems that are not widely publicized. Independent labs and reputable researchers have linked long-term fluoride intake to the following health issues: cancer, genetic DNA damage, thyroid disruption, neurological issues, Alzheimer's disease, and melatonin disruption. The poisonous cumulative effect of sodium fluoride in almost everything we ingest is a cause for concern. Why would the most advanced country in the world not heed the warnings of its own scientific community? Why would we continue to put our children, elderly, and sick at risk? Around 1997, scientist Jennifer Luke studied the effects of sodium fluoride on the pineal gland. She found the pineal gland absorbed the most fluoride, more than any other physical matter, including the bones. She found it calcifies the gland and renders it ineffective in balancing the entire hormonal process throughout the body.

Many communities have come together to eliminate or keep fluoride from the public drinking water system, because people have long believed fluoride is actually slowly poisoning our population in significant ways. While still hotly debated, even most of continental Europe quit putting fluoride in drinking water in the 1970s. Yet fluoridated water still exists in many US communities. Many theories and research exists on both sides. In determining whether to fluoridate for your family, it is always important to do your own research. It is time to listen within to decide what is best for your health and that of your family.

University of Michigan professor of physiology and neurology Jimo Borjigin, who is known as a pioneer in understanding the process of the secretion of melatonin from the pineal gland, states, "We still lack a complete understanding of the pineal gland. Numerous molecules are found in the pineal, many of which are uniquely found at night, and we do not have a good idea of what their functions are. The only function that is established beyond doubt is the melatonin synthesis and secretion at night, which is controlled and modulated by light. All else is speculative." His lab invented long-term pineal microdialysis, which permits automated, computer-controlled analysis of melatonin in rodents. Melatonin is a stunning compound not only found in humans but found naturally in plants, animals, and microbes. His work with the pineal gland seems to link us as humans to the earth's seasons, rotations, and day and night patterns. This study helps us understand how melatonin, which is released during sleep, regulates our bodies to the earth's rotation and nature's time clock. This little gland aligns our natural ability to be in sync with nature, and the release of melatonin at night seems to be an important factor.

While Dr. Borjigin does not refute or support the metaphysical or psychic aspects of the pineal gland, it should also be noted that he has recently found groundbreaking new research. In May 2013, he and his team discovered that dimethyltryptamine (DMT), the chemical known for its psychic connections in the pineal, exists in the pineal gland of live rats. DMT is the chemical released by the pineal that is said to be the catalyst for connecting with the collective consciousness. Pineal calcification interferes with that process.

In 1993 melatonin, which is secreted by the pineal, was also found to be a powerful free-radical scavenger and a wide-spectrum antioxidant that can easily cross cell membranes and the blood–brain barrier. An antioxidant prevents oxidation of cells. Oxidations produce free-radicals, which in turn cause a chain reaction that can eventually kill healthy cells. Melatonin was said to actually work with and improve the overall effectiveness of other antioxidants found in the body that may help with immune disorders, chronic illnesses, and neurologic degeneration. And calcification of the pineal inhibits the amount of natural melatonin released in the body.

A critical study in Chronobiology International: Journal of Biological and Medical Rhythm Research found a definite link between artificial light at night, sleep patterns and cancer. Melatonin is released during darkness and while sleeping. Artificial light disrupts circadian and melatonin secretion, which is clearly linked to high risks of cancer. Up to 120 years ago, humans were exposed on average to twelve hours of sunlight and twelve hours of darkness, give or take location and seasonal changes. But since the invention of the light bulb, we artificially stretch the day, have shorter sleep duration, and even have lights or televisions on while we sleep. All of these affect the function of melatonin in the body. Researcher Itai Kloog states it is easy to fix these detrimental light pollution issues and provides the following suggestions: sleep in a dark room, use less light, and close shutters. He says without a doubt that "with light pollution, we keep paying for and consuming energy resources, night after night, just to re-make this very same pollution, which we could so easily correct if we just put in some effort. In short, stop harming yourself and others in society. Just turn the lights off" (Chronobiology International: Journal of Biological and Medical Rhythm Research).

More stunning research shows that the pineal gland is the only gland in the human body that resembles the visioning elements similar to our eyes. Pineal glands contain a number of things including Pinealocytes which in many non-mammalian vertebrates have a strong resemblance to the photoreceptor cells of the eye. "The pineal of higher vertebrates is not just a simple endocrine gland, rather, its histological organization resembles a folded retina having both hormonal and neural efferentation" (US National Library of Medicine). Some evolutionary biologists believe that the vertebrate pineal cells share a common evolutionary ancestor with retinal cells. In some vertebrates, exposure to light can set off a chain reaction of enzyme events in the pineal gland that regulate circadian rhythms. The third eye represents evolution's earlier approach to photoreception. The structures of the third eye include photoreceptors and retinal cones. The asymmetrical whole consists of the "eye" and the pineal sac or cells believed to be filled with cerebrospinal fluid.

It is amazing that a tiny gland deep in the brain that secretes melatonin and helps enhance antioxidants would also have the properties of a third eye. The notion of the third eye is scientific fact. The purpose of this third eye is the key here, because some believe it opens the door to the metaphysical interpretations of mystical enlightenment and higher states of consciousness, as well as aligning to the third eye chakra.

Some believe the vision aspect of the pineal is where imagination lives in the brain. This vision aspect is the ability to "see" in the mind's eye, to daydream, and to have pictures in your imagination. In fact, melatonin may have a role in the visioning process of the pineal as well, since melatonin secretion increases at night and so does vivid dreaming. Extremely high doses of melatonin, 50 mg or higher, may dramatically increase rapid eye movement enhancing REM sleep time and dream activity. It has also been suggested that hallucinogenic drugs may mimic melatonin activity in the awakened state and that both may act on the same areas of the brain. Others believe DMT may be the catalyst to mimicking hallucinogenic drugs or bringing one into a heightened sense of seeing through the mind's eye.

Everyone can begin healing their pineal gland. Current research shows that rejuvenation of the pineal gland is possible once we remove the detrimental poisons. The most important aspect is your intentional desire to heal the pineal gland. Your thoughts, your conscious intentions, can go a long way in healing the body. We cannot stress enough the power your intentional thoughts and beliefs have on the health of your body.

It would be most beneficial to lower your fluoride intake or avoid everything with fluoride as an additive in it as much as possible. Some researchers say only reverse osmosis and water distillation systems can remove fluoride from drinking water. There are a few brands of toothpaste made without fluoride. Eating organic food, including eliminating genetically modified food and using organic forms of skate oil, which is similar to cod liver oil, can help detoxify the calcium crystals. Consuming items free from preservatives but high in antioxidants is also good for pineal rejuvenation. Raw chocolate and raw cocoa are good pineal gland stimulators. Other specific detoxifiers and stimulants for your discovery include hydrilla verticillata, chlorella, spirulina, blue-green algae, iodine, zeolite, ginseng, borax, D3, bentonite clay, and chlorophyll. There are also specific foods, such as goji berries, cilantro, bananas, honey, coconut oil, hemp seeds, and seaweed that seem to help detoxify and balance the body as a whole. Each of these will require research to determine which might be beneficial to your body. Again, use your intuition and learn what will help you personally.

Spiritual Influences of the Pineal Gland

It is only relatively recently that we have discovered the actual physiological function of the pineal gland, which was just described. However, mystical tradition and esoteric schools have long understood the pineal gland as the connection and link between the physical and spiritual worlds. It is considered the most powerful and highest source of ethereal energy available to humans, and the gateway that leads to inner realms and spaces of higher consciousness. Everyone's pineal gland, or third eye, can be activated toward the frequencies of the spiritual world that enable vision and open the door to a sense of euphoria and oneness. Some believe that with advanced practice and through ancient methods taught in the mystery schools, one can achieve astral travel, astral projection, or remote viewing, all involving the spirit leaving the body. One should not disconnect from the power and the source of spirituality. A closed third eye brings with it confusion and uncertainty. Having a calcified pineal gland can resemble a door being glued shut. It cannot be used while shut, but it is still a doorway. And with continued cleansing, this gland can eventually be opened again.

French philosopher and scientist Rene Descartes (1596–1650 CE) dedicated years to the study of the pineal gland, which he believed was the point of connection between the intellect and the body; the pineal gland is the principle "seat of the soul." What makes the pineal gland so important in terms of consciousness is the vast amount of energy and blood that flows through it, more than any other gland in the human body. The pineal gland is the storehouse of imagination and creation. Descartes believed the physiology to be similar to that of the eyes, allowing the pineal gland to be the place to visualize or imagine scenarios, fantasies, memories, dreams, or any other visual constructs. The expressions, "In the mind's eye", or, "the all-seeing eye," refer directly to the function of the pineal gland.

Cleaning and healing the pineal is necessary for those wishing to develop their multidimensional perception using the body's natural DMT production. DMT consists of carbon, hydrogen, and nitrogen and is a naturally occurring, almost psychedelic drug produced by the pineal. It is present in plants, and trace amounts are also found in the human body. It is a cousin to serotonin. The pineal will naturally make DMT when fully operational, and one can easily tap into a visionary state through discipline and deep meditation. It would seem humans were intended to be visionary beings.

In his book and documentary *The Spirit Molecule,* Dr. Rick Strassman talks about how DMT allows a deeper understanding of reality as we know it. Dr. Strassman started researching DMT in the 1990s. For over twenty years, he studied its hallucinogenic properties and effects in humans. He said he was drawn to work with DMT because of its presence in all our bodies and believed the source of DMT was the mysterious pineal gland. He found that DMT appears in an embryo at forty-nine days into gestation, the same time frame that Tibetans believe the spirit enters the embryo, and around the same time gender is determined. Strassman also found a connection between extreme stress and near-death experiences, where the pineal releases huge amounts of DMT at one time. Strassman says the large amount of DMT in the brain is the cause of the near-death experience phenomenon, where people experience dying, leave their bodies, and then return to their bodies. The pineal gland is considered to be the gateway or star gate within the brain, through which the soul passes as it leaves the body to travel the astral plane during dreaming. And when the body expires or dies, the soul passes through the pineal gland to venture to the higher realms, the soul plane, or a higher dimensional reality.

Strassman administered about four hundred doses of DMT to sixty human volunteers at the University of New Mexico's School of Medicine in Albuquerque, where he was a tenured associate professor of psychiatry. All the participants who artificially received large doses of DMT reported out of body and profound spiritual experiences. Many experiences mirrored those of people who truly did die temporarily and then returned. Almost all experienced meeting a sort of nonhumanoid entity. Participants stated the entities left the participants with a feeling of benevolence. Strassman believes the near-death experiences of the study participants confirm a spiritual existence and the possibility of an afterlife.

DMT is present in the South American shamanic brew called ayahuasca. Ayahuasca is a medicinal tea brewed from the thick, woody stems of the banisteriopsis caapi vine in South America and the big, bushy leaves of the chacruna plant, which is a member of the coffee family. With great reverence, intention, and prayer, the plants are prepared and cooked for eight to ten days. During this time, a shaman sings sacred songs of healing to transform the tea into a sacred medicine. People drink the tea and experience a visionary and spiritual transformation very similar to an experience with peyote or any hallucinogenic drug. Shamans have used this brew for many generations as a way to tap into the spirit world. It is said the practice brings profound physical and heart healing experiences through the purgative effects, which often include vomiting, sweating, and diarrhea. Then it gives the individual the ability to perceive altered states of consciousness and sometimes the experience of other dimensions.

Ayahuasca has been used in religious ceremonies for thousands of years. It should be noted, however, that it is an illegal substance in the United States. Those who use ayahuasca in other countries report they go into a period of "spiritual work" when they use it, where issues about one's life come into awareness and can be healed from the insights they gain from the DMT-like consciousness. Both DMT and ayahuasca allow one to transcend the ego and realize we are one consciousness, giving us the opportunity to rapidly heal our sufferings and conflicts to cleanse our karma. However, with enough practice and development, the pineal gland can produce the key DMT substance on its own and provide the same experience.

Pineal Gland in History

Many ancient cultures make reference to the pineal gland in artwork, adornments, or other relics. They always depict it with the symbol of the pinecone, since the pineal gland resembles that shape. The pinecone is perfectly balanced in sacred geometry, too; the shape and spines spiral in perfect Fibonacci sequence.

The first known references are found on ancient Sumerian tablets, which show sketches of people displaying a pinecone as well as the symbol of an eye often drawn in headdresses or symbols just above their heads. We also find reference on the Egyptian staff of Osiris, dating back to 1224 BCE, which depicts two serpents encircling the staff of Osiris, winding up to meet a pinecone shape at the top of the staff. Scholars believe the serpents represent parallels to the Kundalini, or spiritual energy, which was often shown as coiled serpents rising from the base of the spine to the third eye in the moment of enlightenment. The Hindu deities show interwoven literal and symbolic representations of serpents and pinecones in both drawings and sculptures. Shiva is consistently depicted with hair coiled in the shape of a pinecone, which is interwoven with a serpent around Shiva's head. The Greeks and Romans incorporated the pinecone into their elaborate system of religious beliefs and mythology. For example, Dionysus, later known as Bacchus to the Romans, was continually depicted carrying a staff woven with ivy and leaves and topped with a pinecone. Romans later built an enormous bronze sculpture, three stories high, in the shape of a huge pinecone that today sits directly in front of the Vatican in the Court of the Pinecone. Next to the pinecone statue lies an open sarcophagus at its base, with another statue of a lion, sitting much like the Sphinx, with Egyptian hieroglyphics written on the bottom of the structure. In fact, the pinecone is featured most prominently on top of the sacred staff carried by the pope himself. And the coat of arms of the Holy See, found on the Vatican flag, shows three stacking crowns that look very similar in shape to a pinecone. Some believe the Holy See name refers to the third eye.

Pinecones, believed to be symbolic of spiritual enlightenment, also turn up as sources of illumination in medieval churches in the candleholders, lamps, and in the artwork. One provocative theory is that the pinecone is actually the fruit from the Tree of Knowledge of Good and Evil revealed in Genesis. In the Genesis story Eve eats the apple from the tree. Rather than the literal interpretation of eating the apple by Eve at the urgings of a serpent, perhaps it was a reference to an esoteric experience through the pineal gland and the Tree of Life. It is an interesting concept given the depiction of pinecones and serpents throughout history. Perhaps this is a reference to Eve discovering the link to cosmic consciousness in some way through the pineal gland portal.

Pinecones also regularly appear framed in Freemason octagons and on the ceilings of Masonic lodges as well. In fact, the Freemason sculpture on the side of the Whitehall Building in New York's Financial District shows two enormous, intertwining snakes spiraling up to a pinecone. We see this same reference over and over again in many ancient cultures and secret societies throughout history.

Workings of the Pineal

David Wilcock, who wrote *Source Field Investigations*, shares some amazing insights into the workings of the pineal gland, referencing the interior of the pineal gland as filled with water. Water in the pineal has a liquid crystalline form and exists with the same rods and cones found in our eyes. Like solid crystals, liquid crystals in water can transmit signals. It is believed a repeating pattern of vibrations pulsing through water produces a smooth transmission of energetic information, using water as the conductor. Liquid crystals are flexible and many times more responsive than solid ones. It is possible that during deep meditation, the pineal gland begins to vibrate, and the crystals in the water within the pineal gland begin to transfer information through light particles or possibly the body's biophotons.

Wilcock says the pineal gland is wired into the visual cortex of the brain and also says that the pineal passes more blood through this tiny organ than any other organ in the body. He believes the pineal houses the etheric cord, so if your soul actually leaves the body, the pineal gland is the gateway that not only allows the soul to leave but the anchor that holds it to the physical body. The pineal gland is activated when the lights go out, or darkness happens, and a sort of electromagnetic shield goes up around the gland. This darkness also stimulates the release of melatonin. It is in this state that Wilcock believes that, like the Torus energy, the pineal gland is activated, able to vibrate and actually spin around to move our minds or consciousness from our space-time third-dimensional world to a time-space quantum world. He believes the liquid crystals in the water are the conductors into the time-space world. As the water begins to vibrate and actually flip over or change in some way, you enter the visionary world of your inner self. When this happens, Wilcock says you may feel pressure, or possibly hear buzz tones, or acceleration inside the head. It is also believed that DMT can accelerate this process. While there is no concrete scientific proof of this, what is clear is that something profound happens within the pineal gland and has been recognized in importance throughout history.

Graham Hancock, who wrote *Supernatural*, speaks of his personal experience in taking ayahuasca, the sacred medicinal drink he either drank or smoked many times with shamans in South America in order to experience the spiritual aspects of the soul. He says it is extremely tough on the body, is not fun, and does not taste very good. But it always provided a remarkable experience on a soul level. The first message he received was that the physical body is not what is important; what is important is your connection with the conscious aspect of your self. The experience, says Hancock, puts you in contact with intelligent entities that help you with important lessons and teach you about your life. Almost all people who experience this altered state have contact with a similar entity. All around the world, others report and describe seeing this same female entity in their experiences. She is a great healer and inspiration who makes you want to fix your life, be more loving, and contribute more to humanity.

Many people also speak about entering extraordinary realms and are shown episodes from their own past lives to help them understand who they really are. Hancock was shown his death and what would happen if he did not change some of the negative things happening in his life. He states that having these experiences was life altering, has changed him in profound ways, and his experiences will stay with him forever. As a society many have lost their way, are not connected to Spirit, or do not see themselves connected to each other. Hancock says love is the only way. It is about giving love, not taking it conditionally. He says we need to completely rethink our way of life in order to continue to evolve.

The pineal gland and the heart are important organs that can connect us to the spiritual universe. This is a time for spiritual advancement for all humanity, and learning to use our spiritual gifts is critical. The pineal gland is vital for supporting intuition. Ayahuasca is provocative but is not recommended for use without being in the presence of one experienced in this sort of work. DMT occurs naturally in the body but would not put you into a visionary state unless you were highly enlightened, evolved, and practiced in meditation.

It is especially important in our world today to do your own research in all areas of your life. The time is gone to blindly follow what everyone says is right for you. It is important to discover your own life path, your own sense of spirituality, to go within, and trust your own intuition. This is necessary to evolving spiritually and helps create a better understanding and acceptance of others. Perhaps we could consider moving away from a life centered on the "I am" and move toward the "we are" together, serving others before ourselves. As always, trust yourself, and connect to the love frequency within to manifest your best life now.

Food for Thought

Consider what you feed your body every day. Complete health is important for a healthy pineal gland. Read all labels before purchasing products. Remember that for some substances, it is the cumulative amounts of the toxins in the body that are harmful or potentially poisoning. Your health and that of your family is of utmost importance. We are a society of fast food, processed food, and medications for every pain and ailment. The current states of our air and water are not always the best for optimum health. Research shows most of the additives in food, water, and our environment affect us biologically, mentally, and spiritually. Even if you shop at local health food stores, read all labels.

Try to buy local foods as much as possible and organic foods if you can. It used to be that bread would mold and tomatoes would rot if left uneaten for a week. Now both may sit on your counter for weeks before they break down, and they can remain longer in your refrigerator. This is not natural, and our digestive systems seem to sense this and may react to accumulated toxins through stomach and bowel ailments.

Be discerning about what is right for you and your family's health. Do not assume anyone else is making the correct choices for you. Do all your own research and then decide. Listen to your intuition. Do not simply trust that the food sold at the grocery store is nourishing your body. Be aware and discerning.

Also be discerning about the medications you and your family ingest. Do your own research and understand the full impact medications and their side effects have on the body. Medications can harden, shrink, and calcify the pineal gland, and many over-the-counter medications can have unintended consequences or be overused. Many medications also contain sodium fluoride.

Bless your food and water with thought intention. Thought intention is more powerful than you can imagine. You are sending out a vibration or frequency into the food when you bless it, which can affect the molecular structure for maximum health and nourishment. Send coherent healing frequencies and blessings into your food and water before eating. Our thoughts can create the world around us, and it can also raise the vibration of our food. Praying before a meal has generally been linked to thanking God for our food. It is also possible to send a coherent thought in the love frequency toward your food specifically that can impact the vibration of your food before it is ingested. Send your food healing thoughts of healthy vibration and love for your best health, for the best health of your families, and for the highest nutritional value for your body.

Drink water! Drink water with your meals. Liquid is a conductor and carries healing energy.

CHAPTER 10

Energy and Spiritual Healing

Every day, think as you wake up, today I am fortunate
to be alive, I have a precious human life, I am not
going to waste it. I am going to use all my energies to
develop myself, to expand my heart out to others; to
achieve enlightenment for the benefit of all beings. I
am going to have kind thoughts towards others, I am
not going to get angry or think badly about others.
I am going to benefit others as much as I can.
—Dalai Lama

Energy healing is also known as light or sound healing, psychic healing, and spiritual healing. Many specific programs have been developed that incorporate energy healing. They include Pranic Healing, Reiki, and BodyTalk to name a few. However, some individuals also have the gift of healing through seeing colors, auras, and energy movement. All energy healing involves moving within a person's energy field to interact, remove, exchange, or replace energy to heal someone. This type of healing usually involves the healer using the energy emanating from the hands and enhancing the energy flow around the patient's body to repair disturbances in the human energy field or aura. Improving the flow of energy in one's body supports the body's ability to heal itself. The "laying of hands" has been practiced many times in various cultures over the years. And today, there is a renewed interest in the ancient practices of energy healing. Energy healing of all types is being accepted, researched, and incorporated into alternative healing practice. Optimal healing practice would holistically integrate Western medicine and energy healing to address the whole of the body, mind, and spirit.

> If the head and the body are to be well, you must begin by curing the soul; that is the first thing ... the great error of our day in the treatment of the human body, is that physicians separate the soul from the body (Plato).

Energy healers have long held the common belief that healing happens through the use of the life force energy that exists around all humans. Hippocrates hypothesized that nature itself was the healing energy or vital force of life. He believed that energy, or nature, actually healed the patient, not the doctor.

Pythagoras had a history in healing arts through instituting his harmonic healing in the musical notes he created. He actually developed a mystery school whose universal philosophy covered many topics and believed at its deepest level that reality is mathematical in nature, that philosophy can be used for spiritual purification, that the soul can rise to merge with the divine, and that certain symbols have a mystical significance. All were used to align the body, soul, and spirit. Pythagoreans believed body and mind were united, and they interpreted dreams as part of the healing process. Even in early Christianity, some priests were chosen to be healers. Such priests used both the practice of laying of hands and prayer for healing. Eventually, though, the church no longer supported this type of healing after the conversion of Constantine to Christianity.

In modern times, Edgar Cayce, mentioned in the first chapter of this book as a well-known healer and channeler, went into trances with the intention of diagnosing and healing patients. In this type of healing, the healer establishes an altered state of consciousness to heal. Hands-on energy healing uses intentional thought but does not require establishing an altered state to heal or diagnose. Psychic healing has recently gained in popularity as well. But with all these variations in healing modalities, it is extremely important to remember that legally, only a medical doctor can diagnose or treat a patient.

All human beings have within them the innate ability to develop the nurturing, healing gift using their personal EMF for hands-on energy healing. As a complement to medical and psychological treatment, energy healing can be especially useful for healing emotional traumas held within the body, because the energies of emotional and psychological traumas often manifest into disease and create blocks within the auric field. Energy healing also appears to have a transformative effect on consciousness and significantly reduces the amount of time needed to heal the emotional and psychological issues associated with illness. The most effective healing happens when body and mind are aligned.

In order to develop the healing gift, one must tap into his or her inner source of intuition and connectedness with the universal Source. Practitioners typically meditate regularly, are aware of their personal chakras and energy centers around the body, and regularly clear their auric fields. Clearing the field as a healer is helpful in order to eliminate the transfer of negative energy and blocks between the patient and practitioner. This is usually done with specific thought intention by way of tapping into the coherent energy emitted from the practitioner's heart portal and directing the energy toward the affected energy field of the patient. Using hands to move through affected areas of an energy block as well as the patient's whole body is necessary to balance energy fields. Many practitioners will use their own style or brand of gifts and talents when healing, which may include different modalities, such as the use of crystals, stones, sound, light, or touch.

Healers should be cognizant of the energy thought forms that may adhere to their hands and find ways to cleanse the energy, especially between treatments. Water is one way to both symbolically and physically cleanse energy, and many practitioners wash their hands and arms between treatments. Always call on the white light of protection to surround the treatment room, healer, and patient, as well as assist in the healing process. If one is interested in becoming a healer, finding a group or mentor would be helpful in developing one's talents prior to moving into healing practice. Again, it is critical to remember all energy healing is a complement to any treatment received from licensed doctors.

Pranic Healing is a highly developed and tested system of energy medicine developed by Grand Master Choa Kok Sui. It uses *prana* (Sanskrit for "life force") to balance, harmonize, and transform the body's energy processes. This invisible bioenergy, or vital energy, keeps the body alive. In acupuncture, the Chinese refer to this subtle energy as *chi*. It is also called *ruach*, or the "breath of life" in Hebrew. Pranic Healing is a simple yet powerful and effective system of no-touch energy healing. It is based on the fundamental principles that the body is a self-repairing, living entity that possesses the ability to heal itself. The healing process is accelerated by increasing this life force, which is readily available from the sun, air, and ground to address physical and emotional imbalances. Master Choa Kok Sui says, "Life force energy or prana is all around us and can be tapped as a powerful source of healing energy at any time."

Reiki is a Japanese technique for stress reduction and relaxation that also promotes healing. It is administered by laying on hands and is based on the idea that an unseen life force energy flows through us and is what causes us to be alive. If our life force energy is low, we are more likely to get sick or feel stress. If it is high, we are more capable of being happy and healthy. The word "Reiki" is made of two Japanese words: *rei*, which means "God's wisdom" or the "Higher Power"; and *ki,* which is "Life force energy." So Reiki is actually spiritually guided life force energy.

Many people practice and follow Reiki. The International Center for Reiki Training offers classes for those who wish to become a Reiki master or healer. There is also a Center for Reiki Research that promotes the scientific awareness of Reiki, providing a list of current evidence-based research published in peer-reviewed journals. There are more than seventy hospitals, clinics, and hospice programs that offer Reiki as part of their services. While spiritual in nature, it is not a religion. There is nothing you must believe in to learn to practice Reiki. In fact, Reiki is not dependent on belief at all and will work on a person's energy field whether you believe in it or not.

In the last thirty years, the ancient art of laying on of hands healing has been gaining recognition through the work of modern-day healers and health-care practitioners such as Dolores Kreiger, who wrote *The Therapeutic Touch,* and Barbara Brennan, who wrote *Hands of Light.* Both women and their books have helped bring attention to the numerous beneficial uses of spiritual hands-on energy healing in everyday lives. Applied hands-on healing or remote healing, such as distance healing or prayer, are practiced around the world more frequently than most people may think. These two authors also expand the notion of healing yourself and the importance of interactions, and the power of the heart in healing with friends, family, and lovers. Some individuals may be drawn to energy healing or be gifted as a healer. But everyone has the ability to learn, because everyone has the heart-centered love frequency that impacts the auric energy fields. What is required are some instructions and practice, which have become more available and accessible to the public on an ever-expanding global scale.

One modern-day healer, well known for his psychic healing, is called John of God. This humble man, located in a remote village of Brazil, is changing people's lives in astonishing ways. He has devoted his life to the spiritual healing of millions of people from all over the world. People make a pilgrimage to his primitive, remote clinic. He is very clear about one thing. He says, "I do not cure anybody. God heals, and in his infinite goodness permits the Entities to heal and console my brothers. I am merely an instrument in God's divine hands." Dr. Wayne Dyer, a renowned speaker and author in the field of self-development, knows firsthand the power that exists in this remote jungle village. Dr. Dyer was diagnosed with leukemia but decided to have this unconventional surgery from John of God. He not only believes he was healed but that the entities healing him also put divine love into his being. He believes his leukemia is in remission, and his life has been profoundly changed forever, for the better.

Spiritual healing involves energy work on the chakras, meditation, and the intention to heal within the energy field around the body and heart. It is done specifically with prayer, meditation, and thought intention connected to the heart of the person requiring treatment, often removing blockages and opening the heart portal. Thought intention has very healing qualities when sent in a coherent frequency from the heart of one to the heart of another. Everyone can be a part of their own healing practice. Most of us simply are not aware of how easily we can heal ourselves and others. Many of us are too busy to be purposeful about spiritual practice. Yet if we truly knew that our energy levels and thoughts profoundly affected loved ones and people around us, we might be more intentional about our practice each day. There are two basic, simple ways you can practice your own healing daily and impact the world: prayer and meditation.

"Prayer" is a word typically associated with some form of organized religion, but we are going to use it in a more holistic way. Typically, prayer is speaking with God and asking for help, healing, or another aspect of need. But this type of prayer stems from a place of duality. You separate yourself from God by praying to him outside yourself. You are part of God not separate from God, and, therefore, you are limiting your connection to the powerful healing energy available from inside you. Instead, praying from a place within you, drawing the coherent love energy from within and through you is very powerful. There is a popular phrase, "The divine is in me." This saying makes "me" separate from the divine. If we shift the saying to "The divine *as* me," we begin to remove the separation.

Prayer is a form of energy transfer—a form of energy healing. When you pray or focus energy in a concentrated, coherent way, you are doing several things. You are healing and helping yourself as well as others. You are filling yourself with the golden light and healing love of the universe. The act of loving another, praying for another in love and caring, is a very *giving* act, an act that gives to you as well as to the recipient. As you pray or transfer loving thoughts and healing energy, you must first fill yourself with love. Make yourself the center of that powerful surge of love, which you then send to the recipient, to the person or situation for which you are praying. Love is all. Love has great power and is the best mechanism for sharing energy with the world from the universal Source and the underlying love frequency. Individual prayers, prayer circles, group prayer, or focused thought among healing circles have a profound effect on those receiving and sending the love energy.

Meditation is also a form of energy transfer. Rather than simply focusing within, it is the process of reaching into yourself and tapping into your inner being and the collective consciousness of Universal Spirit to send a powerful coherent wave of love frequency out to the world at large. This process usually happens in the etheric realm during meditation. Sending love out to the world in the EMF includes all of us as we impact the collective consciousness with powerful healing thoughts. This meditation may be used to send healing to specific areas of the world, groups of people, humanity as a whole, or to send healing energy to Gaia, mother earth. This healing work happens in the theta brain wave frequency.

Alternative forms of healing with sound and light, much like chakra healing, can improve the health of your body, especially when it has been impacted by environmental disruptors if you fly frequently, are exposed to radioactive particles, or if you have taken a lot of medication for long periods. Healing with light or sound vibration, called biomagnetic energy or vibration resonance, has also been around for many years as a healing technique, though it is still considered an alternative healing practice. The premise is that everything that exists, from our cells to the cosmos, has a frequency. Some call this frequency resonance, because the frequency vibrates or resonates at a certain tone in the universe, depending on the number of cycles per second it is vibrating, called hertz. Everything vibrates; even a rock vibrates. As we have seen, the body is inundated with man-made frequencies that interfere with the natural vibrations in nature. Energy healing can interface with our natural body vibrations to align them to naturally occurring frequencies with healing properties. For example, if you have a guitar that is out of tune you may use a tuning fork to bring the string back up to pitch. If you put the tuning fork next to the string, it will help guide you to the perfect pitch. When the string is finally vibrating at the same level as the tuning fork, the guitar string may make the tuning fork hum. In the same way, healing frequencies and your body's energies work together to reach the perfect sound and tune the body frequencies.

Light healing was also mentioned earlier in the discussion about clearing chakras, but it is worth mentioning again. It aligns the body energy to balanced light wave frequencies. Through light wave energy, light frequencies integrate with the body's energetic fields to realign the auric body. Light and sound vibrations can also be used together. Sometimes the sound frequencies can be heard with the human ear, and sometimes we cannot hear the frequencies in nature that best align and rebalance our bodies.

One simple example of alignment and rebalance is time spent in nature, where you align with the beauty that surrounds you and feel rejuvenated and peaceful from the experience. Nature is often the tuning fork that helps your body's resonance rebalance and replenish itself. We do this intuitively. Unfortunately, many people today live in urban areas that do not provide many opportunities to tune in to nature, unlike populations long ago. For that reason, using alternative forms of sound and light healing can be even more critical.

We also find that conscious thought impacts the body's healing processes in profound ways. The heart is an electrical organ. The electrical energy from the heart moves into every cell in our body. This electrical field can be measured outside the body. The nervous system is also an electrical system. Most humans generate minute amounts of electrical voltage depending on what is happening in our lives. When our hearts and minds are aligned, a strong, coherent energy is sent out that is more powerful than any of us realize. We can send information out to the universe, but we can also receive messages, like an antenna, from the cosmos. We just need to listen carefully and intuitively to hear. Healers know that quartz crystals can actually amplify our electromagnetic energies and use them to focus thought, manifest or create, and even heal. We can also use stones to amplify and broadcast our thoughts.

Some believe the ultimate vibration frequency of the cosmos or love is 528 hertz and that it is the true musical scale of the universe. Dr. Len Horowitz, author and authority on the 528 hertz frequency says, "The way that the entire universe is constructed is through a musical mathematical matrix composed of nine core creative frequencies. The frequencies of the Solfeggio scale." The 528 hertz is the central note or tone of this very old musical scale and is most remembered in the chantings and songs of the Gregorian monks. Dr. Horowitz shares that studies by NASA show the sun's output contains 528 hertz as kind of a central frequency within it. The 528 frequency can also be found in oxygen as a result of photosynthesis in plants. Horowitz tells us, "The entire botanical world is actually celebrating the 528 hertz which can be found at the heart of everything including sacred geometry and the sounds of laughter, sighing, and yawning." In fact, sound frequencies recently recorded by NASA include what is called the "sounds of Jupiter." These sounds also vibrate close to 528 hertz.

We can observe this frequency in both the sound and light of the universe. The number central to the audio spectrum of creation is 528 hertz, and that number is the same as the visible light frequency of 528 nanometers. The color of this visible light is green. It is the same color we see in the midcolor range of refracted light from a prism. More stunning is the fact that it is the same greenish-yellow color at the heart of the rainbow and the same color green as the heart chakra. There is always an interesting order to the universe. Even plants on earth receive the sun's rays or vibration of light, which is reflected and seen in the plant's chlorophyll, and is also the color green. The colors of the prism, rainbows, and chakras are seen over and over throughout the natural world and universe.

Horowitz also documents the fantastic healing powers of the 528 hertz frequency. The most notable is the ability to repair damaged DNA. His book *DNA: Pirates of the Sacred Spiral*, which was targeted to the electrogenetics community, discussed the implications of genetic tinkering. Electrogenetics is the basis for designing compounds that can interrupt and offset the energy flow in cancer cells and produce their selective destruction. Electrogenetics describes the energy requirements, energy exchanges, and electrical communications that allow gene reactions to occur in the living state. Scientists manipulate the traditional DNA-based genetic code to try to develop cures, rather than keep the energy exchanges intact through frequency. Instead of manipulation, Horowitz suggests the electrogenetics community consider a different philosophy using frequency in DNA repair.

In 2001 Garrnet McKeen Laboratory found a second code that governs energy exchange and is the electronic receiver and transmitter of DNA. When the codes within DNA get out of alignment and can no longer exchange energy, we die. McKeen says that when something is dead, only the first code is left, but living things always have both codes. According to McKeen, much of conventional chemotherapy treatment attempts to alter and break DNA. Some of the drugs are alkylating agents and directly damage DNA to prevent the cancer cell from reproducing. Because these drugs damage DNA, they can cause long-term damage to the bone marrow. In rare cases, this can eventually lead to acute leukemia. McKeen disagrees with this approach, however, and suggests that when DNA is reconnected electronically and thermodynamically, it sort of tunes the channel, if you will, and the energy frequencies begin communicating again. He says research shows reconnected DNA exhibits pulses of an almost musical nature as they vibrate in perfect resonance! The research is compelling and ongoing using frequency healing.

David Icke started working with the 528 frequency many years ago. He said,

> I realized that the right side of the body is controlled
> by the left-brain, and the left side by the right brain and
> that these correspond with our inner male and female

energies. As I took a 528 tuning fork down each side of the body, I could get in touch with the dominant ancestral DNA that comes thru the Mother's side or Father's side of the chromosomes. I would many times get a tremendous imbalance in the sound between the two sides. The purpose of energy work, as many of you know, is to attain balance. For example, if everything is in balance, such as the ph level, the physical body can heal more naturally. It is the same way in our energy bodies. If we can find that energy balance, that equilibrium, where everything aligns or everything comes into synchronization into the rhythm of the dance of life—then healing becomes the natural state. After hundreds of tunings and positive testimonies, I have learned to trust the ancient Solfeggio scale frequencies in the form of tuning forks as a legitimate healing modality (Davidicke.com).

The ability to use frequency healing on the self is quite simple. Our bodies are filled with water, and sound frequency combined with the water in our bodies and cells can be easily maintained.

Dr. Horowitz also supports the work of Dr. Lee Lorenzen from Berkeley, California, who noted the 528 hertz frequency heals damaged DNA. Lorenzen's work is based on the theory that various types of water resonate at different frequencies and that water can be programmed to respond to different frequencies. He knows living cells contain substantial amounts of water and that cells resonate at various frequencies, which can be seen through magnetic resonance imaging (MRI) technology. Lorenzen recognized that water molecules possessed a "memory" and determined he could realign the molecular structure of water to more beneficial frequencies. When his treated water was introduced into the body, the other living organisms were positively influenced at a cellular resonance. He has patented his clustered water for use in healing.

In other research, Lorenzen needed to use water that exceeded the purity required by law for pharmaceutical applications. It was controversial and difficult to garner support from the Food and Drug Administration for this aspect of his work. Perhaps his work surpassed the bounds of current medical technology or perhaps there simply is no money to be made by the pharmaceutical companies without intervention through medication. His process was fascinating and included the exchange of frequencies between groups of molecules to align their vibrations in a healing manner, similar to the alignment accomplished by a vibrating tuning fork. Placing vibrating molecules together created a sympathetic vibration in selected nearby organs. His research showed there is an array of frequencies, all related to harmonics in the major and minor musical scales that affect photosynthesis, mitosis or cell division, and protein synthesis. The frequencies identified through his work have proven to enhance cell repair, cell defense, and to maintain functions in many applications, including but not limited to immune system defense and DNA repair.

John Hutchinson is a well-known researcher and electromagnetic energy expert from Vancouver, British Columbia. He reports that a selection of music taken from the Sounds of Jupiter, recently recorded from NASA, was used to clear pollutants contained in water. The music was played for a small sample of oil-polluted water from the Gulf of Mexico, and the water was miraculously cleared of deadly petrochemicals. Hutchinson's results are unbelievably promising, because they were certified by the Analytical Chemical Testing Laboratory, Inc., of Mobile, Alabama.

The 528 hertz is the miracle note and one of nine core creative frequencies in a perfect circle of sound that animates physical reality. Vibration, frequency, or tone causes something real to happen in each of the above examples. Similar to atomic energy technology, which uses spinning electrons vibrating with electro-resonance, the 528 hertz tone also causes a frequency resonance that has significant effects on all of life as we know it.

Biochemists refer to using the note of C in DNA repair. Today, however, this C is not the same as the note from the original Solfeggio scale. A regular C on today's scales apparently vibrates to a different frequency, but the C of 528 hertz used in DNA repair is documented as part of the original scale of the Solfeggio, according to Horowitz. The differences in the scales exist due to differing tuning methods utilized in ancient times and are not the same as those in general use today. Today's instruments are not automatically tuned to the Solfeggio scale tones. Our current middle C does not match the middle C on the Solfeggio scale of old.

The Solfeggio frequencies are cyclic variations of the numbers 369, 147, and 258. Horowitz believes that each frequency has specific spiritual and physical healing properties. He says the frequency assigned to mi (for miracles) is 528 hertz. According to Horowitz, the original six Solfeggio frequencies and their holistic applications include

UT—396 Hertz—Liberating Guilt and Fear
RE—417 Hertz—Undoing Situations and Facilitating Change
MI—528 Hertz—Transformation and Miracles (DNA Repair)
FA—639 Hertz—Connecting/Relationships
SOL—741 Hertz—Awakening Intuition
LA—852 Hertz—Returning to Spiritual Order

In *Healing Codes for the Biological Apocalypse*, Dr. Horowitz mentions that Professor William Apel,

> researched the origin of what is now called Solfeggio which arose from a mediaeval hymn to John the Baptist. The first six lines of the music commenced respectively on the first six successive notes of the scale, and thus the first syllable of each line was sung to a note one degree higher than the first syllable of the line that preceded it. By degrees these syllables became associated and identified with their respective notes and as each syllable ended in a vowel, they were found to be peculiarly adapted for vocal use.

Eventually, through time, it is believed the church of old slightly changed the key or pitch and no longer used the original Solfeggio scale. Because these new musical tones still held mathematic resonance, which were frequencies capable of spiritually inspiring humankind to be more godlike, the changes in key or pitch affected alterations in conceptual thought as well. The result distanced humanity from Source even further. In other words, whenever you sing a psalm, it is music to the ears. But it was originally intended to be music for the soul as well. The music was also intended to hold all healing properties of the natural world. It is not hard to imagine this, as there are many references to notes, sounds, and incantations opening portals and aligning energies. Even the Keys of Enoch and the Kabbalah hold that the name of God, YHWH, spoken or chanted correctly in original vowel sounds, would open the spirit realm and connect you with Source.

Standard tuning in most of the music produced today is not the C that equals 528 hertz on the Solfeggio scale that nature, water, and the human heart resonates with for producing natural healing. Most of our instruments and music are tuned to a scale that is not necessarily in harmony with the original balancing sounds in the Solfeggio scale. However, if we changed the key in which most instruments are tuned to better align with the older scale, we may once again be in perfect harmony with the frequency of love and the vibration of the cosmos. Some believe this frequency resonates throughout all living things on earth, in nature, and the entire universe.

Proponents of the love frequency resonating at 528 hertz believe the ancients knew healing abilities and natural frequencies aligned with sacred geometry and sound. Think of a drum beating softly while one is outside, and picture the entire natural world swaying to the beat. Picture the sun's rays, the moon's rays, and even the water dancing to the beat, with everything in perfect harmony. This is the possibility of what the world might feel like if we were able to live in peaceful vibration and unity with the universal flow. Is it possible that the frequency of the unified wave field of Oneness of which we all belong may resonate to this love frequency of 528 hertz?

Another important natural healing element is water, which has a compelling use in the healing process. The body is more than 60 percent water, and water is a liquid crystal conductor of both frequency and light. Some believe water and vibration are the keys to healing most of the physical problems in the world, inside and outside the body. Dr. Masaru Emoto, acclaimed researcher on water, demonstrates that frequency has the power to change the formation of water molecules and the design of ice crystals. Emoto's work has shown us that through both frequency input and thought intention, we can change the molecular makeup of water, actually changing it from a disorganized array of crystals in polluted water to beautiful formations with visible messages, as though the water were connected to the conscious Oneness of the universe. Emoto observed amazing results after showing letters to water, showing pictures to water, playing music to water, and praying or using thought intention toward water. Positive thoughts and emotions have much higher vibrations than negative thoughts and emotions and Emoto demonstrated that the two strongest positive thoughts were those of love and gratitude.

Water may be the key. It is a conductor and may send healing frequencies throughout the body as well as within the pineal gland. As noted earlier, the center of the pineal gland is filled with fluid and water. Water responds to other frequencies, to thought, and to music. It can respond in a clear, coherent fashion or one that is scattered and possibly destructive, depending on the stimulus. On the outside we are surrounded by our EMF, and on the inside we are beings comprised of a large percentage of water that carries the frequencies generated down to a cellular level ... all the way to our DNA. We know the coherent love frequency sent out from the heart can influence water in amazing ways. We also know environmental disruptors and negative thoughts influence energy and water.

If thought intention and frequency affect water this way, and if the human brain is 80 percent water and the body more than 60 percent, what influence does the environment have around us daily? If we no longer have our instruments and music tuned to the Solfeggio scale, which was the basis of the sacred Gregorian chants, are we missing an important healing link? Even Nikola Tesla stated, "If you wish to understand the universe, we must think of energy, frequency and vibration" (Washington Times).

Food for Thought

Practice your own healing through thought intention and meditation. Place healing thoughts within your meditations to focus on specific ailments. Trust your intuition about your body and health. When thinking and belief align, you can move mountains and heal.

Clear your auric fields and chakras regularly through meditation, healing chakra videos found on the Internet, or using a healer.

Consider the frequencies of the environment surrounding you. What music, television, or energy drainers are in your midst?

Consider buying a tuning fork. There are several ways to use the 528 hertz frequency. Tuning forks can be purchased for this specific frequency and used to purify the water you drink and food you eat. You can use thought intention to eliminate pollution and use the 528 hertz tone for your highest good. Thought plus belief equals power.

Try carrying a talisman or devise—some way to remind you of your list for engaging in spiritual practice. Every time you see the talisman, for example, think about the things on your list you want to make a habit in your life. Some people believe it is easier to set reminders for themselves during the day to help them remember something new. The reminder could be a timer on a watch, a string on your finger, a particular bracelet on your wrist, or a stone in your pocket. Just place the thought intention in the talisman, and let it gently pull you into the reminder for action or change.

Learn to use effective visualization. Visualization is one way to see what you want. Visualization is like awake dreaming. You create an experience in your mind or see the outcome of something you want to achieve. You can see it happening. Play the given scenario out in your head over and over to bring the event to perfect conclusion, so you can then manifest the scenario into your life. When you put visualization into practice and then recite affirmations with it, it can be the quickest and most powerful way to create a new belief within your subconscious mind. Imagining how the experience will make you feel is also an important aspect for manifesting it in your life. Remember that aligning belief with intent is the most powerful of all. People are quite influential and can choose to become aware and take steps each day to change their personal programming, live in service to others, and share in love for all.

Positive affirmations are another strong way to influence your life. Saying a positive affirmation about something you want to change with all of your belief and free will can make a difference. Simply wanting something to change or waiting for it to change implies that what you want is not currently there. It resides in the future, and that is where it will stay—in the future. Wanting something creates the emotion of lack, because you do not have it yet. You must believe what you want is possible, see it in your mind's eye as already real or as already having happened, and own it. This process takes your desire out of the future and places it in your now, where it can manifest, because it will no longer be a construct of the future. Fill your thought or desire with emotion and feeling. Again, aligning belief with intent is the most powerful. Your ability to initiate change and influence your reality does not happen overnight. It takes time, much like growing flowers in a flowerbed. You may need to water it for weeks before the first leaf pops through the soil. Then you need to tend it, fertilize it, and send it love for the flower to grow. If you quit tending it, the flower will die. It takes time before the first flower blooms, so have patience with yourself, and be consistent in your practice. End all positive affirmations with these words: "Only if it is for my highest good and the highest good of all."

Again, drink a lot of water. Water can rejuvenate, regenerate, carry healing vibrations through the body, and flush toxins as you begin to heal.

CHAPTER 11

The DNA of Divine Living

A small group of thoughtful people could change
the world. Indeed it is the only thing that ever has.
—Margaret Mead

So why are these particular topics blended as one in a book
about spirituality? What is the common element, the thread
that draws them together? The answer is energy, an intelligent
energy that permeates the heavens and the earth. There is a saying,
"As above so below." The beautiful hum of the celestial universe
is the same tune that is played here on earth. The hardest idea to
grasp is that every atom, cell, and thought in your body is wrapped
in its own vibratory song. Every plant, rock, and tree on earth also
has a vibratory song. Even the stars and galaxy are wrapped in
their own songs. Each song exists independently, yet all songs are
the same. You can send your song out from your heart to comfort
and heal another. And our songs comingle harmoniously together
every time we come in contact with each other. Your song is the
intelligent energy that makes up everything in the universe and is
intrinsic and interconnected through your heart portal. You have
the ability to direct it and share it through the love vibration you
send out to each other and humanity as a whole.

Your ability to be connected in this energy and to understand
the ability to use and direct this energy for the good of all humanity
is the purpose of this book. You share the same cosmic energy as the
earth, the stars, rocks, dolphins, everything that lives and grows,

and everything that spins in the universe, including all planets in all solar systems. We are the same cosmic energy. However, our world here on earth and way of life currently is not centered on the flow of universal love. Free will is ours to have, and our freedom is to create as we choose. But in doing so, we also impact others. Collectively, our planet should ring with the ecstasy of joy, love, and abundance for all. Yet globally, many more people are suffering and starving than those who are not. Even those who believe they have achieved abundance often have a sadness or longing in their inner soul. And it is so simple to change that longing for love. There are places to find it, feel it, and share it as discussed throughout this book.

The universe is energy. We are energy molded in human form. All is intelligent consciousness, mathematical in pattern and repetition. We have been so separated from this flow that the channel for our hearts and our thoughts to tune to is like an old analog TV or radio. Mouse ear antennas are needed to catch the right frequency or possibly a larger antenna to receive a clear channel. Even then, the interference is so great that we often miss signals. We need a stronger amplifier. That amplifier is available to us in healthy chakra systems, a healthy pineal gland, and healthy biological systems for clear light or photon communication all the way down to our DNA. Healthy bodies feed strong hearts and a strong mind able to produce coherent conscious thought. It is the cumulative collective alignment of these systems that receives the clearest channel. In fact, it is the alignment of these that allows us to send the most coherent messages, too. The static that exists around the globe keeps the planet physically dense. Drugs, alcohol, and dirty EMFs keep our minds and hearts physically dense as well. There is so much static from technology, negative emotional outrage, and human anguish that the light from Source can barely penetrate.

Focused thought and intention is like a rod that pierces the static cloud cover and allows the rays of light to come through. And like a ray, once the cloud is penetrated, it spreads as far as it can spread. When entire groups send out coherent thought, the cloud is pierced in an even larger way and a greater source for light to penetrate emerges. Even one person alone can make a difference. If we have many individuals sending clear, clean thoughts into the collective, each of them penetrating the static, then suddenly, there are many rays shooting down to earth. That is the goal—to clear the air, clean the heart, clear the head, and heal the body. Then, action from all of us to come together in humanitarian efforts to clean the earth, create sustainable living, healthy food, clear water, and free energy will be needed. We have enough money, enough food, enough energy, enough love for everyone on the planet. All it takes is one light to bring light to the world, but collectively, we can make lasting change for generations to come. We are humans, after all. We have done great things in the past and can do great things again.

Instead, we are spending money and supporting efforts that are working to change the human template and will impact our world in a much different way for generations to come, and with deeper ramifications. One example is genetic research. DNA and genome research have been the focus of heated ethical debates, mystery, and intrigue. It has become a billion dollar business over the last few decades. Though many have strong opinions on genetic manipulation, here we only attempt to share a few points regarding basic DNA, the mysterious "junk" DNA, and some concerns around genetically altered genes.

DNA is the hereditary material containing the genetic instructions used in the development and functioning of all living things. The DNA segments carrying this genetic information are called genes. Nearly every cell in a body has the same DNA, which is located in the cell nucleus, along with biophotons that hold data and communicate, as we have seen. DNA is shaped in a double helix, and its most important property is that it can duplicate or make copies of itself. When cells divide, each new cell needs an exact copy of the complete DNA genetic structure. However, the most interesting aspect of the DNA structure is that scientists can only identify two strands that function together in the human body. The other 95 percent are called "junk DNA" and are sequences of dark matter that do not work because of many years of the evolutionary process. More curiously, new research within the last two years discovered some strands may actually be turned off rather than simply not needed. Through scientific inquiry, research has exposed that only 3 percent of our DNA is wrapped up in the spiraling double helix strand. Some believe that as the Light grows on the planet the torsion energy waves affect our DNA by reorganizing the junk DNA from a two-strand double helix to a twelve-strand helix, which will advance humankind on the evolutionary path in one giant leap.

For many years, junk DNA did not appear to have any discernible function. However, the term "junk" was a bit misleading. Rather than junk, it is now more commonly referred to as "dark matter." This DNA may, in fact, be stored for a critical reason, and researchers have started exploring dark matter with the goal of learning more about it. The human genome has more "off" DNA than any other animal known to date, but researchers do not yet know why. Very simply, genes that are off from the evolutionary process no longer have a possible function and may truly be junk DNA. But the genes that are turned off have a chance of retaining their original function for up to six million years.

Current research also shows these off genes may influence the behavior of the coded genes within DNA in important ways. They have found a relationship between the two. Within the past year, new research has emerged that shows junk DNA plays a critical role in controlling how cells, organs, and other tissues behave. The findings were part of an immense federal project involving 440 scientists from thirty-two laboratories around the world. The *New York Times* published an article in September 2012 that reported on the project, stating,

> They found that most of the changes that affect diseases
> do not lie in the genes themselves; they lie in the switches
> that are found in the junk DNA. In large studies over
> the past decade, scientists found that minor changes in
> human DNA sequences increase the risk that a person

will get those diseases. But those changes were in the junk, now often referred to as the dark matter—they were not changes in genes themselves—and their significance was not clear. The new analysis reveals that a great many of those changes alter gene switches and are highly significant.

What this means is that small changes in the environment can affect each of us differently. The change may alter one of the gene switches in one body but not in another. It is not the gene that creates the difference; it may be in the dark matter and the way a switch communicates with the gene itself. One person may get a disease based on this switch activation, and another may not.

In the meantime, before these mysteries are fully understood, the race to genetic engineering, manipulation, cloning, genetically altered food, and many other developments with powerful ethical implications continue to explode. Jim Watson, an American molecular biologist, and Francis Crick, a British molecular biologist, working together first isolated the double helix structure of DNA in 1953. By 1973 Herb Boyer, recipient of the 1990 National Medal of Science, and Stan Cohen, an American geneticist, were the first to transfer DNA from one species to another and became the first genetic "engineers." They combined their efforts in biotechnology to invent a method of cloning genetically engineered molecules in foreign cells.

In the 1990s, another project began that catalogued all the genes in the human genome. Scientists were fighting so intensely that presidents and prime ministers had to intervene, but the Human Genome Project was launched both privately and publicly. It was an international, scientific research project whose goal was to determine the sequence of chemical base pairs that make up human DNA. This was the breakthrough that triggered controversy about genetic manipulation. But it also created a multibillion dollar industry. Biotechnology transformed the pharmaceutical industry and genetically modified food was the next biggest revolution in agriculture. In food, some are still concerned that a cancer-causing gene in the DNA of a bacterium fused with a food substance and then ingested might be absorbed by the human stomach, which would spread cancer like an infectious disease. However, genetically engineered food is in all our grocery stores today.

Genetically modified organisms (GMO) or engineered food and plant seed have been on the market for at least twenty years. One of the most contested debates today is the long-term effect of splicing food seed with pesticides and bacteria, something that has been going on for a long time. In fact, there are seven main food crops that are almost completely genetically modified. Margie Kelly, communications manager at Healthy Child, Healthy World, writes about the seven main crops as of October 2012, and the percentages have increased as of 2013.

1. Corn: Corn is the number one crop grown in the U.S. and nearly all of it, 90%, is genetically modified. In addition to being added to innumerable processed foods, genetically modified corn is a staple of animal feed.
2. Soy: About 93% percent of soy is genetically modified. Soy is a staple of processed foods under various names including hydrogenated oils, lecithin, emulsifiers, tocopherol—a vitamin E supplement, and proteins.
3. Cottonseed: According to the USDA, 94% of cotton grown in the U.S. is genetically modified. Cottonseeds are culled from cotton, and then used for vegetable oil, margarine or shortening production, or frying foods, such as potato chips.
4. Alfalfa: Farmers feed alfalfa to dairy cows, the source of milk, butter, yogurt, meat and so much more. Alfalfa is the fourth largest crop grown in the U.S., behind corn, soybeans, and wheat, though there is no genetically engineered wheat on the market, yet.
5. Papaya: Over 75% of the Hawaiian papaya crop is genetically modified to withstand the papaya ringspot virus.
6. Canola: About 90% of the U.S. canola crop is genetically modified. Canola oil is used in cooking, as well as biofuels.

In North Dakota, genetically modified canola has been found growing far from any planted fields, raising questions about what will happen when "escaped" modified canola competes with wild plants.

7. Sugar Beets: More than half, 54%, of sugar sold in America comes from sugar beets which are 97% modified. Genetically modified sugar beets account for ninety percent of the crop; however, that percentage is expected to increase after a USDA's decision last year gave the green light to sugar beet planting before an environmental impact statement was completed.

So if you have any crackers, cereals, cookies, snack bars, soy milk, baby formula, or anything with corn syrup, you are probably consuming GMO foods. And now small amounts of zucchini and yellow squash sold in the United States are genetically modified. GMOs are plant or meat products that have had their DNA altered in a laboratory by genes from other plants, animals, viruses, or bacteria. They actually splice the two DNA genes together, altering them forever. We then ingest them into the body. For example, genetically modified corn now contains a pesticide in its DNA structure.

Research, especially research from the UK and other European nations, link GMOs to allergies, organ toxicity, and other health issues. The Food and Drug Administration does not require foods that are genetically modified to be labeled, because it considers these foods equivalent to regular crops, however some states today are taking the matter into their own hands. Groups are fighting for labeling laws, so consumers have the right to choose whether to purchase modified food for their families, especially children or the elderly. However, supermarket chains have up to 70 percent of processed foods on their shelves that are made from at least one of the seven crops above, so they support the efforts to not label foods. As in the sodium fluoride example, it is the cumulative health effect of these chemicals in our systems and the long-term unintended consequences that are the issue.

Much of current research deals with the unintended effects of genetically modified crops that go beyond the original modification and that might impact health and the environment. Results show that new genotypes invade natural ecosystems and cause undesirable and permanent change. The potential risk is caused by "the processes of transgene insertion or rearranging DNA with other plants, animals or pesticides" (Journal of Applied Ecology). Modified crops may have an impact on surrounding natural soil, bee populations, natural crop contamination, and other effects that may permanently change our food supply. It is up to us to make a difference and review all available research, as well as consider who funded the research and what they found.

Unintended health effects are also a major concern. Many of today's doctors were not taught about "leaky gut syndrome" in medical school, yet many symptoms in children and adults seem to lead to this unconventional diagnosis. When a food like corn is spliced with a pesticide, it kills a potential insect during the growth process by ingesting the pesticide inside the growing kernel and bursting the insect's stomach from the inside out. Now some researchers believe the unintended consequence is the same chemical reaction happening over time within the intestinal walls of humans. While not bursting from the inside out, they believe it is possible that small holes appear in the intestinal lining that cause stomach acid to leak out of the intestines. This causes a whole host of problems. While it is difficult to prove the connection completely, the reality is since GMO food and meat products have been introduced into human consumption in the last twenty years, digestive diseases like Crohn's disease, colitis, and diverticulitis have risen dramatically. This has also led to a plethora of new medicines for the big pharmaceutical companies to sell. As always, it is critical to do your own research here, especially if you or a family member has any symptoms or diseases in food allergies, stomach issues, or digestive problems that may be affected by diet.

Research already shows the impact of our environment on the pineal gland and other aspects of our precious body chemistry. We truly do not know the long-term health effects of eating foods that have been genetically modified. Nor do we know the long-term effects on our food supply or the delicate balance of nature. What we do know is that the beautiful balance of our natural world and our amazing biological body systems are affected daily. Even Jim Watson, who discovered the DNA structure some sixty years ago, holds shocking and controversial views of how to apply this knowledge. He was quoted as arguing for a new kind of eugenics, where parents were allowed to choose the DNA of their children to make them healthier, more intelligent, and even better looking. What are the consequences of the next evolutionary process of the human race? And if our "off" DNA holds ancient information for us as a human race, how might gene manipulation affect this precious process of discovery? We live in a critical time where our next steps in the evolutionary process could be important for the world we leave our children and grandchildren. We must be in charge of our own lives from an informed perspective and choose what is best for our families, rather than blindly following the lead of corporations and big business. Take time to stay abreast of critical issues facing our world. We are an interdependent global world, and our choices affect all of humanity.

As you proceed on your spiritual path, connecting to Source daily, more frequency changes and more light will be directed into your body. With more light comes more data, all the way down to the cellular level. You may feel surges of energy during the day, and you will need to direct them intentionally. When you begin to separate yourself from the day-to-day dramas and observe things from outside the emotional realm, you may find you need to ground yourself more often. Simply walking outside and being in nature helps ground you during the day. Like nature, bloom where you are planted; grow wherever life takes you. The ability to keep our antennas clear and increase the vibration of love that comes in and out of our body is dependent on our physical health as well as the health of our souls. Put your heart and soul out into the cosmic field, and nurture it daily. There is an aura of electro light energy that extends for a mile around the physical body. Conscious intention extends information into this field and receives vibrations back.

It will take all of us to advocate for a better world. If we each choose something we are passionate about, learn about it, and place it in our conversations, sharing it with others, we may be able to make a difference for all humanity. We each have gifts and talents we can share to help cocreate a better world for everyone.

There will always be a paradox in your life; you will continually have choices to make. Ultimately, it really makes no difference what choice you make, because it will always create more choices and more choices. If you do not like the path you are on, you have the power and free will to change it. The only constants are to honor your relationships, send love to the world, and directly connect to Source daily. Emotions influence subconscious behavior, and negative emotional attachments require intention to fix and change. So intentionally send out love, even to those who may have hurt or wronged you in some way. Let it go, or it will manifest into energy blocks in your body—or worse, disease. As you begin to see energy at work in your life and see evidence of the connected power of the universe, you will suddenly observe your life objectively and see clearly your power and how to govern your own existence. Your choices will become clear, and your world will hold a sense of peace that emanates from within. Your beautiful connection to Source can spread to others near you and eventually envelop all in joyful love. And you will be living a centered spiritual life.

Do unto others as you would have done to you. Again, all that really matters is our connection to Source and each other. Take care of your "self" and your health, and give to the good of all humanity. To get love you must give love to the world. Be love, and you will reap multitudes back. In the end, we are all one, and we are one with God/Source/All That Is!

'Tis in ourselves that we are thus or thus. Our bodies
are our gardens to which our wills are gardeners.
—*Othello*, by William Shakespeare

Bibliography

"A Brief Synopsis of Research Regarding Clustered Water." *Cluster Plus.* Retrieved August 22, 2013. http://steamteam.ca/wpcontent/uploads/2012/08/ClusteredWaterSynopsis1.pdf.

Anodea, Judith. "The Chakras." *Sacred Centers.* Retrieved July 20, 2013. http://sacredcenters.com/chakras-and-asana-practice/#.

Anthony, Sebastian. "The First Quantum Entanglement of Photons through Space and Time." *ExtremeTech* (May 24, 2013). Retrieved July 14, 2013. http://www.extremetech.com/extreme/156673-the-first-quantum-entanglement-of-photons-through-space-and-time.

Artson, Rabbi Bradley Shavit. *God of Becoming and Relationship: The Dynamic Nature of Process Theology.* Woodstock, VT: Jewish Lights Publishing, 2013.

Bailey, Regina. "Pineal Gland." *Biology About.* Retrieved July 22, 2013. http://biology.about.com/od/anatomy/p/pineal-gland.htm.

Barnstone, Willis. *The Other Bible: Gnostic Scriptures, Jewish Pseudepigrapha, Christian Apocrypha, Kabbalah, Dead Sea Scrolls.* San Francisco: Harper & Row, 1984.

Barnstone, Willis, and Marvin Meyer. *Essential Gnostic Scriptures.* Boston: Shambhala Books, 2010. 271.

"Biophoton Communication: Can Cells Talk Using Light?" *Technology Review* (May 22, 2012). Retrieved July 15, 2013. http://www.technologyreview.com/view/427982/biophoton- communication-can-cells-talk-using-light/.

Bischof, Marco. *Biophotons—The Light in Our Cells*. Frankfurt: Zweitausendeins May, 1998. http://www.zweitausendeins.de/.

Bradley, Michael. *Secrets of the Freemasons*. New York, NY: Sterling Publishing, 2008.

Brennan, Barbara. *Hands of Light: A Guide to Healing Through the Human Energy Field*. New York, NY: Bantam Books, 1988.

Brook, Robert D., Lawrence J. Appel, Melvyn Rubenfire, Gbenga Ogedegbe, John D. Bisognano, William J. Elliott, Flavio D. Fuchs, Joel W. Hughes, Daniel T. Lackland, Beth A. Staffileno, Raymond R. Townsend and Sanjay Rajagopalan. "Beyond Medications and Diet: Alternative Approaches to Lowering Blood Pressure: A Scientific Statement from the American Heart Association." *National Library of Medicine National Institutes of Health* (April 22, 2013). Retrieved July 13, 2013. http://www.ncbi.nlm.nih.gov/pubmed/23608661.

Burstein, Dan. *Secrets of Mary Magdalene*. Durham, NC: CDS Books, 2006.

Cayce, Edgar. "On Oneness." *ARE Clinic*. Retrieved June 14, 2013. http://www.edgarcayce.org/are/edgarcayce.aspx?id=3558.

"Cell Phones and Cancer Risks." *National Cancer Institute*. Retrieved December 30, 2013. http://www.cancer.gov/cancertopics/factsheet/Risk/cellphones.

"Cellular Resonance Water." *Aqua Technology*. Retrieved August 7, 2013. http://www.aquatechnology.net/frame43179.html.

"Chakras." *Crystalinks*. Retrieved July 20, 2013. http://www.crystalinks.com/chakras.html.

"Chakras." *The Chopra Center*. Retrieved July 20, 2013. http://www.chopra.com/community/online-library/terms/chakras.

"Chakras." *Of the Light*. Retrieved July 20, 2013. http://www.ofthelight.net.

"The Chakra Guide: Harness the Power of Your Chakras." *Gaiam Life*. Retrieved July 20, 2013. http://life.gaiam.com/article/harness-power-your-chakras.

Champagne, Pascale, and C. S. K. Mishra. *Biotechnology Applications*. New Delhi, India: IK International Publishing House, 2009.

Chemiske, Steve. "Aqua Resonance: Clustered Water, a Summary of the Work of Dr. Lee Lorenzen." *Mednat.org.* Retrieved July 22, 2013. http://www.mednat.org/bioelettr/Aqua%20Resonance.pdf.

Chester, Marvin. *Primer of Quantum Mechanics.* Hoboken, NJ: John Wiley & Sons, 1997.

Connett, Paul. "50 Reasons to Oppose Fluroidation." *Fluoride Action Network.* Retrieved July 22, 2013. http://www.fluoridealert.org/articles/50-reasons/.

Crane, Gregory. "Greek Science and the Library of Alexandria." *Ancient Worlds: The Egyptian World.* Medford, MA: Tufts University, 1995. Retrieved August 5, 2013. http://www.ancientworlds.net/aw/Article/1161774.

"Create Reality Using Your Thoughts—Scientifically Proven Methods." *Quantum Jumping.* Retrieved August 28, 2013. http://www.quantumjumping.com/articles/parallel- universe/creating-reality/.

Daulby, Martin, and Caroline Mathison. *Guide to Spiritual Healing.* London: Brockhampton Press, 1996.

Dawkins, Richard. *The Selfish Gene.* 2nd ed. London: Oxford University Press, 1989.

Dewey, David. "Introduction to the Mandelbrot Set." Retrieved July 18, 2013. http://www.ddewey.net/mandelbrot/.

De Witt, Bryce, and Niel Grahm, eds. "The Many-Worlds Interpretation of Quantum Mechanics." *Princeton Series in Physics.* Princeton, NJ: Princeton University Press, 1973.

"DMT Found in the Pineal Gland of Live Rats." *Cottonwood Research Foundation, Inc.* (May 23, 2013). Retrieved August 12, 2013. http://www.cottonwoodresearch.org/dmt-pineal-2013/.

Douglas, Nik. *Spiritual Sex: Secrets of Tantra from the Ice Age to the New Millennium.* New York, NY: Simon & Schuster, 1997.

"Einstein." *History Channel.* (February 2013). Retrieved July 10, 2013. http://www.youtube.com/watch?v=P8DrxzkwnmA.

"Electrogenetics." *Garnett McKeen Laboratory* (2001). Retrieved August 7, 2013. http://www.facr.org/pdf/ELECTROGENETICS-Summary-from-web-1.pdf.

Emoto, Masaru. *The Hidden Messages in Water*. New York, NY: Atria Books, 2005. http://imprints.simonandschuster.biz/atria.

Emoto, Masaru. "What is the Photograph of Frozen Water Crystals?" (Retrieved July 29, 2013). http://www.masaru-emoto.net/english/water-crystal.html.

"Energy Healing Research using Bio-Magnetic Energy." *Natural Cleansing Techniques*. Retrieved August 10, 2013. http://www.naturalcleansingtechniques.com/energy-healing.html.

Evans, Jules. "Spiritual Healing." *Scientific and Medical Network* (July 14, 2008). Retrieved August 5, 2013. https://www.scimednet.org/sapphire/main.php?url=/spiritual-healing-2/.

Eves, Howard. *An Introduction to the History of Mathematics*, 6th ed. Independence, KY: Cengage Learning, 1990.

"Fibonacci Sequence." *Science World at Telus World of Science*. Retrieved July 18, 2013. http://www.scienceworld.ca/fibonacci.

"Fluoride & the Pineal Gland: Study Published in Caries Research." *International Fluoride Information Network, Bulletin 260* (March 27, 2001). Retrieved August 10, 2013. http://www.redicecreations.com/specialreports/fluoridepinealgland.html.

"Forgotten in Time: The Ancient Solfeggio Frequencies." *Red Ice Creations* (January 21, 2006). Retrieved August 4, 2013. http://www.redicecreations.com/specialreports/2006/01jan/solfeggio.html.

Freeman, Lyn. *Mosby's Complementary & Alternative Medicine: A Research-Based Approach*. 3d ed. London: Mosby Elsevier, 2008.

Freke, Timothy, and Peter Gandy. *The Hermetica*. London: Judy Piatkus Ltd., 1997.

Gabriel, Linda. "Exploring the Power of the Mind from Science to Spirituality." *Thought Medicine*. Retrieved July 10, 2013. http://thoughtmedicine.com/2010/07/.

Gerber, Richard. *Vibrational Medicine: The #1 Book on Subtle-Energies Therapy*, 3rd ed. Rochester, VT: Bear & Company, 2001.

The Gnosis Society, 3363 Glendale Blvd., Los Angeles, CA 90039. http://www.gnosis.org.

Goleman, Daniel. *Emotional Intelligence*, 10th ed. New York, NY: Bantam Books, 2005.

Graham, Gordon. *Genes: A Philosophical Inquiry*. New York: Routledge, 2002.

Gray, A. J., and Alan F. Raybould. "Genetically Modified Crops and Hybridization with Wild Relatives: A UK Perspective." *Journal of Applied Ecology* 30, no. 2 (1993).

Griffiths, David J. *Introduction to Quantum Mechanics*. 2nd ed. Upper Saddle River, NJ: Prentice Hall, 2004.

Hancock, Graham, and James Tyberonn. "Exploration of Consciousness: An Interview with James Tyberonn" (December 2012). Retrieved February, 2013. http://www.youtube.com/watch?v=A2395HLF4Yw.

Hecht, Laurence. "The Solar Storm Threat to America's Power Grid." *21st Century Science & Technology* (June 13, 2011). Retrieved July 2, 2013. http://www.21stcenturysciencetech.com/Articles_2011/Solar_Storm_Threat.pdf.

Heylighen, Francis, and Klaas Chielens. "Evolution of Culture, Memetics." *Encyclopedia of Complexity and Systems Science* (2009).

Horowitz, Leonard G. *The Book of 528: Prosperity Key of Love*. Pearblossom, CA: Medical Veritas International Inc., 2011.

Horowitz, Leonard G., and Joseph E. Barber. *Healing Codes for the Biological Apocalypse*. Las Vegas, NV: Healthy World Distributing, 1999.

"How do Electromagnetic Fields Affect Melatonin Production?" *Yahoo Voices*. Retrieved August 10, 2013. http://voices.yahoo.com/how-electromagnetic-fields-affect-melatonin-production-7667418.html.

Hulse, David D. *A Fork in the Road: An Inspiriting Journey of How Ancient Solfeggio Frequencies are Empowering Personal and Planetary Transformation!* Bloomington, IN: AuthorHouse, 2009.

Hurtak, James J. *The Book of Knowledge: The Keys of Enoch*. Los Gatos, CA: Academy for Future Science, 1977.

Icke, David. "Repairing Your DNA—with 528 HZ Frequency." Retrieved August 2, 2013. http://www.davidicke.com/forum/showthread.php?t=20512.

"The Importance of Oxygen." *Natural Cleansing Techniques*. Retrieved August 10, 2013. http://www.naturalcleansingtechniques.com/oxygen.html.

"Indigenous Native American Prophecy Parts 1, 2, and 3." Retrieved June 7, 2013. http://www.youtube.com/watch?feature=player_embedded&v=g7cylfQtkDg#at=51.

"Is Dirty Electricity Making You Sick?" *Prevention* (November 2011). http://www.prevention.com/health/healthy-living/electromagnetic-fields-and-your- health?page=7.

Johari, Harish. *Chakras: Energy Center of Transformation*. Rochester, VT: Destiny Books, 2000.

Jonas, Wayne B., and Cindy C. Crawford. "Science and Spiritual Healing: A Critical Review of Spiritual Healing, 'Energy' Medicine, and Intentionality." *Alternative Therapy Health Medicine* 9(2).

Kaku, Michio. "String Theory." *MKAKU.org* (December 2011). Retrieved June 28, 2013. http://www.youtube.com/watch?v=kYAdwS5MFjQ.

Kappenman, John. "Geomagnetic Storms and Their Impacts on the U.S. Power Grid." *ORNL.gov* (January 2010). Retrieved July 4, 2013. http://web.ornl.gov/sci/ees/etsd/pes/pubs/ferc_Meta-R-319.pdf.

Kloog, Itai, Boris A. Portnov, Hedy S. Rennert, and Abraham Haim. "Does the Modern Urbanized Sleeping Habitat Pose a Breast Cancer Risk?" *Chronobiology International: The Journal of Biological and Medical Rhythm Research* (February, 2011). Retrieved December 27, 2013. http://informahealthcare.com/doi/abs/10.3109/07420528.2010.531490?journalCode=cbi

Knott, Ron, and Douglas A. Quinney. "The Life and Numbers of Fibonacci." *Pass Maths +Plus Magazine*. Retrieved July 18, 2013. http://plus.maths.org/content/life-and-numbers-fibonacci.

Kolata, Gina. "Bits of Mystery DNA, Far from 'Junk,' Play Crucial Role." *New York Times*, September 5, 2012.

Krieger, Dolores. *Therapeutic Touch Inner Workbook*. Rochester, VT: Bear & Company, 1996.

Lacroix, Nitya. *Kama Sutra: A Modern Guide to the Ancient Art of Sex*. New York, NY: Hylas Publishing, 2003.

Lawlor, Robert. *Sacred Geometry: Philosophy & Practice (Art and Imagination)*. London: Thames and Hudson 1982. Retrieved August 12, 2013. http://www.scribd.com/doc/8320/Robert-Lawlor-Sacred-Geometry-Philosophy-and- Practice-1982.

Lesser, George. *Gothic Cathedrals and Sacred Geometry Vol.I*. London: A. Tiranti, 1957.

Little, Gregory, Lora Little, and John Van Auken. *Edgar Cayce's Atlantis*. Virginia Beach, VA: A.R.E Press, 2006.

L/L Research. *The Law of One Books II, III, and IV. Ra, a Humble Messenger of the Law of One*. Atglen, PA: Whitford Press, 1982.

Liboff, Richard L. *Introductory Quantum Mechanics*. Old Tappan, NJ: Addison-Wesley, 2002.

Mangasarian, Mangasar M. "The Martyrdom of Hypatia (or The Death of the Classical World)." Speech before the Independent Religious Society, Chicago, May 1915. http://www.polyamory.org/~howard/Hypatia/Mangasarian.html.

Marciniak, Barbara. *Bringers of the Dawn: Teachings from the Pleiadians*. Rochester, VT: Inner Traditions/Bear Publishing, 1992.

Mark, Joshua J. "Alexandria." *Ancient History Encyclopedia 2011*. Retrieved August 15, 2013. http://www.ancient.eu.com/alexandria/.

"Massive Solar Flare Could Paralyze Earth in 2013." *Science Tech* (September 21, 2010). Retrieved July 2, 2013. http://www.dailymail.co.uk/sciencetech/article-1313858/Solar-flare-paralyse-Earth-2013.html.

McTaggart, Lynne. *The Field: The Quest for the Secret Force of the Universe*. New York, NY: Harper Perennial, 2008.

"Meditation Breathing Techniques." *Squidoo*. Retrieved July 22, 2013. http://www.squidoo.com/meditation-breathing-techniques.

Mehra, Jagdish, and Helmut Rechenberg. *The Historical Development of Quantum Theory*. New York, NY: Springer-Verlag, 1982.

Michaelson, Jay. *Everything is God: The Radical Path of Nondual Judaism*. Mt. Vernon, WA: Trumpeter Publishing, 2009.

Morris, Steven M. "Achieving Collective Coherence: Group Effects on Heart Rate Variability Coherence and Heart Rhythm Synchronization." *HeartMath, Alternative Therapies in Health and Medicine* (2010).

Mowry, Scott. "The Ancient Solfeggio Frequencies—'The Perfect Circle of Sound'. Love Transformationl Tools #9." *Miracles and Inspiration.* Retrieved August 6, 2013. http://www.miraclesandinspiration.com/solfeggiofrequencies.html.

Muir, Charles, and Caroline Muir. *Tantra: The Art of Conscious Loving.* San Francisco, CA: Mercury House Publishers, 1989.

"High Altitude Electromagnetic Pulse (HEMP)." *Navy Department Library* (August 20, 2004). Retrieved August 17, 2013. http://www.history.navy.mil/library/online/hemp_hpm.htm.

"New Study Furthers Einstein's 'Theory of Everything'." *Physics.org* (February 8, 2013). http://phys.org/news/2013-02-furthers-einstein-theory.html.

Oakes, Lornia, and Lucia Gahlin. *The Mysteries of Ancient Egypt.* London: Lorenz Books, 2003.

Oschman, James. *Energy Medicine: The Scientific Basis.* London: Churchill Livingston, 2000.

Pagels, Elaine. *Beyond Belief: The Secret Gospel of Thomas.* New York: Vintage Books, 2003.

Pagels, Elaine. *The Gnostic Gospels.* New York: Random House, 1979.

Pagels, Elaine. *The Gnostic Gospels.* New York: Vintage Books, 1989.

Pagels, Elaine, and Karen L. King. *Reading Judas: The Gospel of Judas and the Shaping of Christianity.* New York: Viking Press, 2007.

Pangman, M. J., and Melanie Evans. *Dancing with Water: The New Science of Water.* Coalville, UT: Uplifting Press, 2011.

Peniel, John. *The Children of the Law of One and The Lost Teachings of Atlantis* (1997). Retrieved June 12, 2013. http://www.scribd.com/doc/5368989/Edgar-Cayce-the-children-of-the-law-of-one-and-the-lost-teachings-of-atlantis.

Pennick, Nigel. *Beginnings: Geomancy, Builder's Rites, and Electional Astrology in the European Tradition.* London: Capall Bann, 1999.

Pennick, Nigel. *Sacred Geometry: Symbolism and Purpose in Religious Structures*. London: Capall Bann, 2001.

Phillips, Tony. "Giant Breach in Earth's Magnetic Field Discovered." *NASA Science News* (December 16, 2008). Retrieved July 4, 2013. http://science1.nasa.gov/science-news/science-at-nasa/2008/16dec_giantbreach/.

Pope, Timothy. *Healing from the Heart*. Retrieved July 17, 2013. http://www.healingfromtheheart.co.uk/69701.html.

Quick, Susanne. "Delving into Alternative Care: Non-Traditional Treatments Draw Increased Interest, Research Funding" (October 17, 2004). Retrieved July 14, 2013. http://www.highbeam.com/doc/1G1-123525955.html.

Ramsdale, David, and Cynthia W. Gentry. *Red Hot Tantra: Erotic Secrets of Red Tantra for Intimate, Soul-to-Soul Sex and Ecstatic, Enlightened Orgasms*. Pankenham, ON: Quiver Publishing, 2004.

"Rapid Detoxification of the Third Eye (Pineal Gland)." *The Healers Journal*. Retrieved July 22, 2013. http://www.thehealers journal.com/2012/12/17/rapid-detoxification-of-the-third-eye-pineal-gland/.

Rawles, Bruce. *The Geometry Code: Universal Symbolic Mirrors of Natural Laws Within Us*. Castle Rock, CO: Elysian Publishing, 2012.

Rich, T. R. "Judaism 101: What Do Jews Believe" (2011). Retrieved June 8, 2013. http://www.jewfaq.org/beliefs.htm.

Rosch, Paul J., and Marko S. Markov. "Chapter: Clinical Applications of Bioelectromagnetic Medicine." In *The Energetic Heart: Bioelectromagnetic Communication Within and Between People*. New York, NY: Marcel Dekker, 2004.

Rueckert, Carol. *The Law of One Parts 1, 2, and 3*. Retrieved June 9, 2013. http://www.youtube.com/watch?v=y79dX5SJHDY.

Saraswati, Swami Sivananda. *Kundalini Yoga*. Tehri-Garhwal, Uttarakhand, India: Divine Life Society, 2005.

Schuld, Andreas. "Green Tea, Fluoride & the Thyroid. An Open Letter to Susan Cameron-Block 1999." *Current Health Issues*. Retrieved August, 14, 2013. http://poisonfluoride.com/pfpc/html/green_tea.html.

"Second Thoughts about Fluoride, Reports Scientific American" (January 2, 2008). *Reuters*. Retrieved August 13, 2013. http://www.reuters.com/article/2008/01/02/idUS108377 +02-Jan-2008+PRN20080102.

"Severe Space Weather Events—Understanding Societal and Economic Impacts: A Workshop Report." *The National Academies Press* (October 24, 2012). Retrieved July 2, 2013. http://www. nap.edu/catalog.php?record_id=12507.

"Shamanic Retreat—Ayahuasca." *Heart of the Initiate*. Retrieved August 10, 2013. http://www.heartoftheinitiate.com/workshops/ colombia-ayahuasca.

Sheahen, Laura. "Matthew, Mark, Luke and ... Thomas? What Would Christianity Be Like if Gnostic Texts had Made it into the Bible?" *Beliefnet* (June 2003). Retreived August 31, 2013. http://www.beliefnet.com/Faiths/2003/06/Matthew-Mark-Luke-And-Thomas.aspx.

Skinner, Steven. *Sacred Geometry: Deciphering the Code*. New York: Sterling, 2009.

Smith, Jeffery. *Genetic Roulette: The Documented Health Risks of Genetically Modified Food*, 4th ed. Portland, ME: Yes! Books, 2007.

"Solfeggio Frequencies." *Sonalkiss Research*. Retrieved August 4, 2013. http://sonalkiss.com/solfeggio-frequencies/.

Strassman, Rick. *The Spirit Molecule: A Doctor's Revolutionary Research into the Biology of Near Death and Mystical Experiences*. Paris, ME: Park Street Press, 2000.

Swerdlow, Stewart A. "Creating Your Reality: All You Need Is Your Mind." *Huffington Post* (July 10, 2012). Retrieved August 2, 2013. http://www.huffingtonpost.com/stewart-a- swerdlow/ creating-your-realityall-_b_1649933.html.

Theopedia. http://www.theopedia.com/Gnosticism.

Thill, Scott. "4 Things You Should Know About Your 'Third Eye'." *AlterNet*. Retrieved July 23, 2013. http://www.alternet. org/personal-health/4-things-you-should-know-about-your-third-eye.

Turner, John D. "Nag Hammadi Codex XIII." In *Nag Hammadi Codices, XI, XII, XIII*, edited by Elaine H. Pagels and Charles W. Hedrick, p. 363. Boston: Brill, 1990.

Tyberonn, James. "Footprints in the Sand." *Earth Chronicles* 81 (April 7, 2013). http://www.earth-keeper.com.

Tyberonn, James. "The Law of Attraction: When & How it Works & Why It Sometimes Doesn't, Part One." *Earth-Keeper Chronicles* 63 (August 13, 2011). http://www.earth-keeper.com/EKchronicles_63pdf.pdf.

Tyberonn, James. "The Law of Attraction: When & Why It Works & Sometimes Doesn't, Part Two." *Earth-Keeper Chronicles* 64 (September 23, 2011). http://www.earth- keeper.com/EKchronicles_64pdf.pdf.

Tyberonn, James. "The Law of Attraction: When & How it Works & Why It Sometimes Doesn't, Part One Modified." *Earth-Keeper Chronicles* 65 (December 26, 2011). http://www.earth-keeper.com/EKchronicles_65pdf.pdf.

Tyberonn, James. "Revisiting Atlantis: The Crystalline Field of 10-10-10." *Earth Chronicles* 46 (June 6, 2010). http://www.earth-keeper.com/EKchronicles_46pdf.pdf.

Van Auken, John. *Edgar Cayce and the Kabbalah*. Virginia Beach, VA: A.R.E. Press, 2010.

Vigh, B., MJ Manzao, A. Zdori, CL Frank, A. Lukats, P. Rohlich, A. Szel, and C. David. "Nonvisual Photoreceptors of the Deep Brain, Pineal Organs and Retina." *US National Library of Medicine*. Retrieved December 27, 2013. http://www.ncbi.nlm.nih.gov/pubmed/11962759.

Vigh, B., A. Szel, K. Debreceni, Z. Fejer, MJ Manzano e Silva, and I. Vigh-Teichmann. "Comparative Histology of Pineal Calcification." *US National Library of Medicine*. Retrieved December 27, 2013. http://www.ncbi.nlm.nih.gov/pubmed/9690142.

Weinberg, Steven. *Dreams of a Final Theory: The Search for the Fundamental Laws of Nature*. London: Hutchinson Radius, 1993.

"What Is Timing, and Why Is It Important in Astronomy?" *Goddard Space Flight Center, NASA*. Retrieved August 7, 2013. http://imagine.gsfc.nasa.gov/docs/science/how_l2/timing.html.

Whirling Rainbow Foundation. Retrieved June 7, 2013. http://whirlingrainbow.com/who-we- are/whirling-rainbow-prophecy/.

White, David Gordon. *Kiss of the Yogini*. Chicago, IL: University of Chicago Press, 2003.

Wilcock, David. "David Wilcock Explains the Pineal Gland." Retrieved July 19, 2013. http://www.youtube.com/watch?v=W4oO_xVfreM.

Wilcock, David. "David Wilcock Interviews Graham Hancock" (January 2008). Retrieved July 19, 2013. http://www.youtube.com/watch?v=WvNEVvHgOOY.

Wurtman, Richard, and Julius Axelrod. "The Pineal Gland." *Massachusetts Institute of Technology*. Retrieved August 13, 2013. http://wurtmanlab.mit.edu/static/pdf/40.pdf.

Yogananda, Paramahansa. *Autobiography of a Yogi*, 2nd ed. Nevada City, CA: Crystal Clarity Publishers, 2003.

Zimmer, Carl. "DNA Double Take." *New York Times*, September 16, 2013.

Lightning Source UK Ltd.
Milton Keynes UK
UKOW02f1207190916

283315UK00001B/209/P